Durham Bi
Volume One

edited by G. R. Batho

Durham County Local History Society
2000

Introduction

Council of the Society has decided to publish a series of volumes, of which this is the first, of potted biographies of men and women who made a significant, but not necessarily a high profile, contribution to the life of the region as defined by the boundaries of pre-1974 County Durham and industrial Tyneside and Teesside in the nineteenth and twentieth centuries, or who were residents and achieved fame outside the region. It is intended to have a cumulative index in subsequent volumes.

The Society is grateful to the contributors and invites anyone who wishes to contribute to later volumes to contact me.

G. R. Batho
Honorary Editor

Emeritus Professor G. R. Batho, School of Education,
University of Durham, Leazes Road, Durham, DH1 1TA,
tel: 0191 386 8908   fax: 0191 374 3506.
e-mail: G.R.Batho@durham.ac.uk

DEDICATION

David Sturrock Reid (1906–1998)   **Adult educationalist**

D avid Reid was born on 27 December 1906. He was the only son of
parents who farmed at Blairgowrie in Perthshire where the family was
long settled. He attended Harris Academy in Dundee and then went to the
University of St Andrews where he graduated with first class honours in
Modern and Mediaeval History. He was moreover distinguished in his year
at St Andrews as Medallist in Modern History. He won a Carnegie
Scholarship and did research at the Institute of Historical Research in
London for his doctorate. This he obtained in 1934 at St Andrews for his
thesis, 'British Public Opinion on Anglo-American Relations, 1783–1794'.
He was clearly well qualified by student achievement as well as by
temperament and preference to take up an academic career. For the next
twelve years, this was not to be.

His father had died before the First World War and it appears that
inheritance of the family farm made it necessary for him to take up farming,
immediately upon completing his doctorate. This he did for the next six
years, 1934–40, although he made time to obtain the post-graduate diploma
in Business Administration at the Dundee School of Economics in 1939.
When the war intervened, he first assisted the principal of the Dundee
School who had become the city's food executive officer and then had a five
month stint in 1940 as an official censor in Liverpool, where he learnt to
fathom the pious code of Irish exiles writing home, – G.W.: God Willing, –
etc.. Then he volunteered for the RAF where he obtained a commission and
became an intelligence officer. War service took him to North Africa, to
Italy, and France. He took part in all the landings in the Mediterranean
theatre of war. Some of these were very violently contested but he would
only speak of that in southern France which, according to his report, was an
unchallenged tour of liberated wine cellars. He would tell too of having to
refuse the gift of a small girl from a North African Arab he had unwisely
complimented as her father; or of being given a jeep by an American
serviceman in Naples when he was stranded after a night out. Among his
effects, is a notebook in which occur a number of intelligence summaries,
such as the following for 1943:

> ... 27/28 Sgt Miller 2130 vectored NE on to raids flying from N.E.
> climbed to 8,000 ft. ... orbited to intercept and on 230° made contact
> to starboard at maximum range and almost immediately obtained
> visual on 3 a/c identified as JU88s 2,000 ft above and 10,000 ft

ahead. Climbed and saw 3 other Ju 88 ahead. followed close then saw 6 more to starboard and 6 to port and 3–6 behind. all in echelon starboard formations. Chose an outside a/c of nearest 3 and closed to 300 ft behind and opened firing button, checked safety catch. Cannons on "fire" Banged with fist and short splutter resulted but nothing more. Ju 88s dived away but not before opening fire which however went wide.

... Rest of the Ju 88s also turned and dived away. This took place some 5m North of Philippeville at approx 1945 hrs.

... Ag 15 During the day a German P/W a Sgt Flt engineer was brought to the mess. He was one of a Ju 88 crew shot down by F/O Mellish DFC on Ag 10 and picked up from the sea by a N.Z. merchantman after swimming in Mae West for 32 hours. P.W. was quite talkative.

... Ag 25 Some German refuelling equipment allotted to the squadron was collected from Catania. From first inspection this equipment seems very efficient and in certain points superior to ours e.g. in lightness of construction and super filtering arrangements. The fact that the trailer has metal wheels may be indicative of rubber shortage.

In 1946 David was appointed WEA tutor-organiser for Dundee, Angus and East Perth. Then in 1948, he was appointed staff tutor in History and International Relations in the department of Extra-Mural Studies at Durham University. He came to play an influential and responsible part in the Durham department's administration, as senior tutor from 1961. H. J. Boyden, Tom Daveney and John Dixon, directors throughout David's period in the department, valued his opinions and advice. Tom Daveney has said he could not have moved without him and all knew they could rely absolutely on his confidence. In 1956, the Foreign Office invited him to lecture to Volkshochschulen in West Berlin as part of a programme to rehabilitate the study of History in West Germany.

As a tutor in Durham, he soon came to play a part in the development of the study of Local History which first developed as an academic subject in the post-war period. It was struggling for acceptance rather as was the history of his own country, Scotland. Both Local and Scottish History really only began to flourish from the 1960s. David was in the first generation of those who not only taught but promoted Local History as a subject. He also built up the departmental library, and until he went in 1972, it was a first class history library. He bought widely and discriminatingly.

He played a principal part in founding the Durham County Local History Society in 1964 and became its first chairman. He thought Durham history was then too much that of the archaeological and ecclesiastical periods and that there was the need to correct an imbalance with the new history of social and economic perspectives from the 16th century – and to the 19th. He was always very sure that was the chief aim of the society and maintained that view with firmness. He made a very material contribution to the history of the county in the book he wrote and published as recently as 1990, on the Durham Crown Lordships, showing how commercialisation of rents was at least as important as enclosure in the transformation of the agricultural economy and the role of what might be termed the public sector, of the Durham Crown lands, in that process. It is a very good book which deserves to be known widely as an exemplary study. It was well reviewed.

He was a most companionable man but lived alone. He was a bachelor but very definitely heterosexual in his preferences, – elegance was a quality which attracted him in women. He was very appreciative of the company of friends and was an excellent host. He enjoyed going to "raise food", as he put it, for an occasion, and "hooch" as well. He had a small collection of pictures which included an original etching by J. M. W. Turner and another by Raoul Dufy; lithographs by Juan Gris and Georges Braque, Marc Chagall and Fernand Leger; and original paintings and watercolours by Paul Marny, John Varley, Sir David Wilkie, Tom McGuiness and Norman Cornish. He played the piano with *brio*. His repertoire was exclusively classical. He particularly enjoyed listening to opera. He was a very expert and diligent gardener, making imaginative and knowledgeable use of the small areas to the front and back of his house. Until his sixties, when he turned to somewhat more conservative marques, he drove Rileys and Jaguars.

He was pre-eminently a reasonable man, a man of liberal opinions. There was in his liberalism not a little anti-clericalism, not obsessional but there are all same. He was very conscious of the religious and regional tensions of his Scottish homeland but regarded them with something approaching amusement. He would often speak of a Highland and Island tour he made in his university days, with a friend, a fellow-student at St Andrews, the American writer, James A. Michener, who had the habit of Americans of those days, of putting his glass quickly under a chair when a door opened. They passed from one valley of stern weefrees into the next of libertine papists, people mutually suspicious and never meeting. David was fortified in his opinion that enthusiasms were dangerous. On admission to hospital in his final illness, he was asked his religion and promptly gave the old soldier's answer, "C of E", confiding later that it was the answer which saved most trouble.

In his will he was extremely generous to friends and to the institutions which nourished him and which he served. He made very generous bequests to the two universities, St Andrews and Durham. He was most generous, too, to the Durham County Local History Society. He was always particularly anxious that the Society should produce a biographical series and it is now gratifying that we may dedicate this series to him in grateful and affectionate memory.

H. J. Smith

David Reid

William George Armstrong (1810–1900)   Industrialist

William George, later Baron Armstrong of Cragside, lived from 1810 to 1900. Born in Newcastle upon Tyne, the son of a wealthy corn merchant, he studied law in London and returned to Newcastle to practise in the established firm of Armorer Donkin.

Increasingly frustrated with law, he turned to scientific studies. Electricity was his first love, and exponents like Faraday and Wheatstone were among his supporters. Evidence of this prowess is seen at Cragside, the home he designed near Rothbury in Northumberland, which was the first house in the world to be lit by hydro-electricity.

In 1847 he purchased a 5-acre site at Elswick, then a little village west of Newcastle quayside. From the outset, he showed his concern for the education of his employees by developing a Mechanics' Institute on the site.

Soon he moved into that sphere for which he has become most famous – armaments. Appalled by the fact that the British Army was content to use the same weapons in the Crimean War as they had done at Waterloo, some 40 years earlier, Armstrong used modern techniques and materials to produce a much lighter, more manoeuvrable, breech loading gun with a rifled barrel and a shell for a projectile. Although this was derided by the Army as a mere 'pop gun', nonetheless, Armstrong was knighted for his efforts and made Engineer of Rifled Ordnance at Woolwich, with the remit to equip the Army with his modern guns.

Despite his success, his rivals and even the Government reneged on their promises and returned to the old fashioned muzzle loading guns. In consequence, Armstrong resigned his Government appointment and returned home.

As the Works continued to expand and diversify, first into ordnance then into shipbuilding, Armstrong sought new challenges. Realising the importance of scientific and technical education, he commissioned John Dobson to design a new Mechanics' Institute at Elswick which was upheld as the blueprint for the Government's plans for scientific and technical education.

Meanwhile, back in 1863, having recently returned from Woolwich a disillusioned man, he was accorded what he described as, 'The greatest honour of my life.' When the British Association for the Advancement of Science met in Newcastle for only the second time, they invited him to be their president. Other presidential appointments quickly followed, and these addresses reflect a visionary more in tune with the ideas of our own day than of his own. He spoke of the finite nature of fossil fuels and of the need for alternative energy sources like waterfalls and solar power. He recognised the advantage of centrally heated homes; of metrication and of a Channel Tunnel.

Realising that the classical curricula of Oxbridge and Durham Universities were inadequate for the aspiring scientists of the day, he fully supported the development of the College of Physical Science in Newcastle. Later the Durham University College of Science, it became, on his death, Armstrong College of Science. Shortly before World War II, it merged with the Newcastle based Durham University College of Medicine to become King's College, Durham University. Now, as part of Newcastle University, it is still known as the Armstrong Building.

Armstrong's philanthropy to his native city was as wide ranging as it is legendary. His scientific interests are reflected in his support of the Hancock Museum and of the Newcastle Literary and Philosophical Society.

Nonetheless, his character as the true educator emerges at the Society's Centenary Lecture when Armstrong, as President, spoke about his recent electrical researches. Looking at the apparatus he had used to illustrate his lecture, he observed:

> "But there will be some among you who will say: 'Of what use are such experiments as these?' The answer is that the more we pry into the mysteries of electricity, the more we shall be able to apply it to the service of mankind. But, apart from that consideration, knowledge, for knowledge sake, is a worthy subject of pursuit!"

Bibliography

A. I. Short, 'The Contribution of William, Lord Armstrong, to Science and Education', Ph.D. thesis, University of Durham, 1989.

The Scientific Research Papers and Presidential Addresses of Lord Armstrong and the Original Records and Log Books of the Elswick Works' Literary and Mechanics' Institute and the Elswick Works' Schools, by kind permission of Messrs. Vickers' Defence Systems PLC Elswick, Newcastle upon Tyne.

Royal Commission, Select Committee and other Reports.

Reports of the British Association for the Advancement of Science in the

National Library of Scotland, Edinburgh, Queen Margaret University College, Edinburgh, the Universities of Edinburgh, Heriot Watt, Durham and Newcastle upon Tyne.

Records in the library of the Literary and Philosophical Society of Newcastle upon Tyne.

Records of the College of Physical Science, Durham University, and the University of Durham College of Science, the University of Newcastle upon Tyne.

A. I. Short

The Backhouse Family   Bankers and Horticulturists

The Backhouses were a Quaker family, and several of them became highly regarded naturalists and horticulturists. James Backhouse (1721–1798), founded the Backhouse Bank in Darlington, Co. Durham in 1774, with his sons Jonathan (1747–1826) and James (1757–1804). Jonathan Backhouse afforested the poorer land on his estates at Weardale in Co. Durham, an undertaking that was continued by three of his four sons. Jonathan (1779–1842), (better known as a supporter of the Stockton–Darlington Railway), Edward (1781–1860), (founder of the Backhouse Bank in Sunderland) and William (1779–1844) were all awarded medals by the Royal Society of Arts for their enterprise.

However, William Backhouse was not just a forester, being well known as a botanist in the north of England. He had close contact with Nathaniel John Winch (1768–1838), the Newcastle-based botanist, to whom he forwarded a list of rare Durham plants in February 1805. William was particularly interested in British grasses and cultivated specimens sent to him by friends and correspondents. He died suddenly at a Friends Meeting in Darlington in June 1844. Sadly Backhouse's herbarium, considered of real scientific merit, was destroyed by fire when on loan to J. G. Baker, in 1865.

William Backhouse senior had two sons and three daughters. The eldest son, William Backhouse II (1807–1869), continued the family interest in botany, became a competent entomologist, ornithologist, geologist and meteorologist, and developed a number of new varieties of *Narcissus*. William junior worked in the branch of the Backhouse Bank established in Newcastle in 1825 and he became a founder member of The Natural History Society of Northumberland, Durham and Newcastle upon Tyne in 1829. A competent entomologist, William made extensive notes on Lepidoptera captured on the Backhouse estates in Durham and his fascination with meteorology is revealed in diaries devoted to daily temperature and weather reports, and in requests from correspondents for readings from his 'Weather Gauge'. Surviving water-colour drawings of local coastal sections, and extensive transcriptions, indicate his knowledge of geology. He had a collection of stuffed birds, and showed promise as an artist, producing water-colours, engravings and pencil drawings of a variety of subjects. When William returned to the Darlington Bank, he lived at St. John's Hall, near Wolsingham, Co. Durham and here he began his major horticultural work, the development of new varieties of *Narcissus*. Following his death in 1869 his daffodil collection was purchased by Peter Barr and used in association with that of Edward Leeds (1802–1877) to establish a classification system for narcissi.

Robert Ormston Backhouse produced the first pink-trumpet daffodil, which he named 'Mrs R. O. Backhouse' after his wife

Three of William's four sons from his second marriage, (to Katherine Aldam (1815–1868) in 1843), Charles, Henry and Robert, kept up the family interest in daffodils. Charles James Backhouse (b. 1848) continued to live at St. John's, whilst Henry Backhouse (1849–1936) reared daffodils in

Darlington from 1895–1907 and in Bournemouth from 1907–1925. William Backhouse II's youngest son, Robert Ormston Backhouse (1854–1940) married Sarah Elizabeth Dodgson in 1884, and two years later moved to Sutton Court, Sutton St. Nicholas, Hereford. Continuing the family interest in narcissi, Mrs. R. O. Backhouse (1857–1921) achieved national fame, being awarded the Royal Horticultural Society's Barr Cup in 1916. In 1923 Robert astounded the horticultural world with the first pink-cupped, white perianthed daffodil which he named 'Mrs. R. O. Backhouse'. His son, William Ormston Backhouse (1885–1962), worked for a period of five years at the Cambridge Plant Breeding Station and the John Innes Institute, but left Britain to become a geneticist for the Argentine Government. He established a number of wheat-breeding stations in Argentina, then moved to Patagonia, where he reared pigs, grew apples and other fruits and started intensive honey production. W. O. Backhouse obtained narcissi from his parents, and in South America continued the family tradition set by his grandfather. He specialised in red-trumpeted daffodils, and on his return to England and Sutton Court in 1945, continued to develop these varieties.

The banker James Backhouse (1757–1804) married Mary Dearman of Thorne, Yorkshire. Their sons Thomas Backhouse (1792–1845) and James established the Backhouse plant nursery in York. James Backhouse I (1794–1869) is arguably the most famous of all the Backhouse naturalists. He was educated in Leeds, but on his return to Darlington he began to explore nearby Teesdale with the lead miner John Binks (1766–1817), who is credited with the discovery of many of the rare plants in Teesdale. Binks, the Newcastle botanist Nathaniel John Winch, and William Hooker (1785–1865) were all major influences on James Backhouse, as indeed were his uncle Edward Robson (1763–1813) and his cousin William Backhouse (1779–1844).

James Backhouse and his brother Thomas purchased the York nursery of John and George Telford in 1815, and made it a great success. However, James was an active missionary, and on 3 September 1831, in the company of George Washington Walker (1800–1859), he boarded the *Science*, bound for Australia. He stayed in the country until 1838, carrying out missionary duties and humanitarian work, but also collecting plants and seeds which he sent back to the York nursery and to Hooker in Glasgow. On the return journey he visited Mauritius en route for South Africa, where he stayed until December 1840, finally arriving back in York on 21 February 1841. Backhouse described his travels in two books, his *Narrative of a visit to the Australian Colonies* (1843) and *Narrative of a visit to the Mauritius and South Africa* (1844), both illustrated with engravings by Edward Backhouse

(1808–1879) of Sunderland, from original sketches by the author. Hooker and William Harvey (1811–1866) recognised the value of Backhouse's botanical observations, naming a Myrtle *Backhousia* in 1845.

Throughout his Australian journey Backhouse had been in correspondence with his son James Backhouse II (1825–1890). From 1843 father and son explored Upper Teesdale and other mountainous areas of Britain and Europe in search of alpine plants. They jointly directed the growth of the York nursery from 1845 on the death of Thomas Backhouse, supervising its move to a 100 acre site at Holdgate, York in 1853. James Backhouse II wrote a *Monograph of the British Hieracia* (1856) and in the pages of *The Phytologist* recorded his botanical discoveries in Teesdale and other mountainous areas of Britain.

James Backhouse II was also a keen archaeologist and geologist; he explored the caves of Teesdale in search of archaeological material and with his son, James Backhouse III (1861–1945) formed a small private museum. The Teesdale Cave was excavated by the James Backhouses II and III between 1878 and 1888; these explorations are described in James III's *Upper Teesdale Past and Present* (1896). He had close connections with the Yorkshire Museum, York, being an active member of the Yorkshire Philosophical Society, and an Honorary Curator of Zoology; the museum holds James Backhouse III's collection of cave material and some 4,000 bird skins. James III is best known as an ornithologist and as the author of the *Handbook of European Birds* (1890). In 1891 he formed a new company, Backhouse Nurseries (York) Ltd., which faced considerable competition from other plantsmen. Most of the land was sold in 1921 and the nursery finally ceased trading in 1955.

Edward Backhouse (1808–1879) was the son of Edward Backhouse (1781–1860), founder of the Sunderland branch of the Backhouse Bank. A philanthropist, artist, pioneer photographer and historian, he is best known for *Early Church History* and other religious works. Fascinated by natural history, he built significant zoological, botanical, archaeological and ethnographic collections which were transferred to Sunderland Museum in 1907. Edward Backhouse's nephew Thomas William Backhouse (1842–1919) of West Hendon House, Sunderland, built an observatory there. His recordings of the weather and movements of the stars gave him considerable standing as a meteorologist and astronomer. He began to compile his 'Astronomical Journal' in 1858, which eventually extended to 36 volumes, and published a series of 14 maps of stars, accompanied by *A Catalogue of 9842 Stars Visible to the Naked Eye* (1911); the star maps were completed after his death. Thomas Backhouse's accurate meteorological observations were uninterrupted from 1857–1919, and his work was recognised by the Royal Meteorological Society, who appointed him as Vice-President in 1918 and 1919.

Bibliography

E. Backhouse, & C. Taylor, *Early church history to the death of Constantine*, London, Hamilton Adams & Co., 1884.

J. Backhouse, *A narrative of a visit to the Australian colonies*, London, Hamilton Adams, 1843.

J. Backhouse, *A narrative of a visit to the Mauritius and South Africa*, London, Hamilton Adams and Co., 1844.

J. Backhouse, Jnr., *A monograph of the British Hieracia*, York, Simpson, 1856.

J. Backhouse, Jnr., 'Teesdale botany: historical and personal recollections', *Naturalist*, 10, 10–13, 1884.

J. Backhouse, III, *A handbook of European birds for field naturalists and collectors*, London & York, Gurney and Jackson, Wm. Sessions, 1890.

J. Backhouse, III, *Upper Teesdale past and present*, London & Barnard Castle, Simpkin, Marshall, Hamilton, Kent & Co., W. R. Atkinson, 1896.

S. Backhouse, *Memoir of James Backhouse by his sister*, York, Wm. Sessions, 1870.

T. W. Backhouse, *A Catalogue of 9842 stars visible to the naked eye for the epoch of 1900*, Sunderland, Hills and Co., 1911.

W. Backhouse, 'Additions to Mr. Hogg's catalogue of birds observed in south eastern Durham and north western Cleveland, with some observations thereon', *Newman, Zoologist*, 4, 1261–1263, 1846.

W. Backhouse, 'Letter on the hybridisation of *Narcissus*', *The gardener's chronicle and agricultural gazette*, June 10, 530, 1865.

G. W. Bain, 'Early days of banking in Sunderland', *Antiquities of Sunderland and its vicinity*, Vol. 6, pp. 76-94, 1905.

J.G. Baker, 'Biographical notes on the early botanists of Northumberland and Durham', *Transactions of the Natural History Society of Northumberland*, 14, 69–86, 1903.

E. A. Bowles, *A handbook of Narcissus*, London, Martin Hopkinson, 1934.

P. Davis, 'William Backhouse (1807–1869) of St John's Hall, Wolsingham: entomologist, ornithologist and horticulturist', *Naturalist*, 112, 85–93, 1987.

P. Davis, 'James Backhouse of York (1794–1869): missionary, traveller and botanist', *Archives of natural history*, 16, 247–260, 1989.

P. Davis, 'The Backhouses of Weardale, Co. Durham, and Sutton Court, Hereford; their botanical and horticultural interests', *Garden history*, 18 (1), 57–68, 1990.

T. C. Dunn, 'Entomologists', in Lunn, A. G., (editor), *A history of naturalists in north east England*, Newcastle upon Tyne, Department of Adult Education, University of Newcastle upon Tyne, 1983.

J. Foster, *The descendants of John Backhouse, Yeoman, of Moss-side, Yealand Redman, Lancashire*, London, privately printed at the Chiswick Press, 1894.

G. G. Graham, *The flora and vegetation of County Durham*, Durham Flora Committee and the Durham County Conservation Trust, 1988.

J. Harvey, *Early nurserymen*, London & Chichester, Phillimore, 1974.

B. R. Hillard, 'An appreciation – Mr. W. O. Backhouse – breeder of daffodils', *Gardeners chronicle*, October 27, 305, 1962.

R. Howse, 'Catalogue of the fossils of the Permian System of the Counties of Northumberland and Durham, drawn up at the request of the Tyneside Naturalists' Field Club, *Transactions of the Tyneside Naturalists' Field Club*, 1, 219–264, 1848.

J. Jacob, 'Mrs. R. O. Backhouse – in memoriam', *The garden*, 19 February, 96, 1921.

J. S. Jeans, *Jubilee memorial of the railway system. A history of the Stockton and Darlington railway and a record of its results*, London, Longmans Green & Co., 1875.

M. Phillips, *A history of banks, bankers and banking in Northumberland Durham and North Yorkshire, illustrating the commercial development of the north of England from 1755–1894*, London, Effingham, Wilson and Co., 1894.

A. Raistrick, *Quakers in science and industry*, Newton Abbott, David & Charles, 1968.

J. Robinson, 'Sunderland banks and bank notes', *The Library Circular, Sunderland*, 1 (5 January), 1900.

J. Robinson, 'Sunderland worthies no. 6 – Edward Backhouse', *The Library Circular, Sunderland*, 1 (8 October), 1900.

J. E. Robson, 'A catalogue of the Lepidoptera of Northumberland, Durham and Newcastle upon Tyne', *Transactions of the Natural History Society of Northumberland*, 12, 1–318, 1902.

C. Simms, 'Change and no change; survival of Backhouse material in the north east of England', *Journal of the Society for the Bibliography of Natural History*, 7, 369, 1976.

H. Spencer, *Men that are gone from the households of Darlington*, London & Darlington, C. A. Bartlett, Rapp & Dresser, 1862.

'Visitor', 'Messrs. Backhouse & Sons nurseries at York', *Garden and forest*, August 20, 403–404, 1890.

F. Watson, *The Backhouse family of Darlington*, Sunderland Library (typescript in Local Studies Section), 1962.

Thomas Watson, & Sons, *Auction catalogue; The library at Morland, Abbey Road, Darlington, Co. Durham*, Darlington, Watson, 1978.

D. Wheeler, 'The work of Thomas Backhouse, Victorian meteorologist', *Weather*, 38 (8), 240–246, 1983.

W. Wilks, 'The renaissance of the daffodil in Britain', *Daffodil year book*, 1933.

H. T. Wood, *The history of the Royal Society of Arts*, London, Murray, 1913.

Peter Davis

Florence Eveleen Eleonore Bell (née Ollife) (1851–1930)   Author

Florence Ollife was raised in Paris where her father, Sir Joseph, was physician at the British Embassy. Her family's circle of friends was cosmopolitan and the youthful Florence an accomplished musician. She was nineteen when she moved to England because of the Franco-Prussian War. Six years later she became the second wife of Hugh Bell, son of the great

North-East ironmaster Isaac Lowthian Bell. The couple settled at Red Barns, Redcar, a house designed for Lowthian Bell by the architect Philip Webb, a close associate of William Morris. It is an interesting indication of the character of the new mistress of the house that Webb should have been recalled to design, among other additions, a bicycle shed – cycles being regarded at the time both as new-fangled inventions and as an un-ladylike mode of transport.

Florence Bell had entered a different world to that of Paris and fashionable London and she set about exploring it – and not just on a bicycle. At Bell's Port Clarence ironworks a special railway wagon was fitted-out with upholstered swivel chairs and porthole windows to permit her and her guests discretely to view men at work. From the early 1880s, Florence Bell led a small team of 'female visitors' who called on ironworkers' wives, offering advice and discreet support to those in need of it. Through this medium she gathered much material she would later put to telling use in the book for which almost exclusively she is remembered, *At the Works: A Study of a Manufacturing Town* (1907). Ostensibly about Middlesbrough, subsequent research has established that much of the book concerns Port Clarence on the north bank of the Tees.

Florence Bell's considerable output as an author, however, was dominated by works of a very different character. Her publications include three French language primers, four novels and six 'jest books' – games and light reading for country house parties. She had eight plays produced on the London stage, wrote the 1921 York Minster Pageant and countless essays and articles. Some of the latter appeared in the French academic journal *La Science Sociale*. Although her contributions to the latter were on educational issues, they seem to have stimulated her critical awareness of social questions generally and to have widened her awareness of the French sociologists Comte and Le Playe, whom she obliquely quoted in *At the Works*.

However, *At the Works* is not a rigorous sociological analysis (wherein lies, perhaps, a clue to its enduring readability). Florence Bell was an accomplished writer, exhibiting more than a little of the prose style of Charles Dickens, whom she had known in her youth. Yet she wrote with a very clear understanding of contemporary social and political context. Her main source of sociological inspiration was Charles Booth, whose pioneering *Life and Labour of the London Poor* (1891–1903) was a landmark study and to whom *At the Works* is dedicated. Bell was noticeably cooler about the work of her other great contemporary Seebohm Rowntree, whose research into York, *Poverty: A Study of Town Life*, was published in

1901 and which the title of her own book surely consciously evoked. However, the difference in the two titles is illuminating, Rowntree's starkly emphasising poverty, Bell's no less emphatically stressing work and manufacturing. Herein lies a clue to her political views and silence upon the ostensible contradictions of her own position. The latter puzzles and even infuriates some readers. Her husband, after all, employed more than 6,000 in South Durham and Cleveland, yet her investigations never refer to the level of wages as a contributing factor to the poverty she found.

Florence Bell espoused (discreetly, as she believed a wife should do) the free market politics of her husband. They held to a strongly individualistic concept of *laissez-faire* liberalism which by the Edwardian period was being eroded from all sides – by progressive liberalism, tariff reform Toryism, and Socialism. In particular the Independent Labour Party was strong in Middlesbrough, whilst in 1892 Hugh Bell, standing as a Liberal-Unionist, had been defeated by a Labour candidate in the fight for the borough's parliamentary seat. Both the title and chapter organisation of *At the Works* were surely intended to remind readers of the source of family incomes and the general wealth of the community alike. Belief in the dynamism of a free market economy meant that she held fast to an outlook which had no room for any concept of fundamental social reform. In contrast to Rowntree, who used his study of York to argue the case for old age pensions, Florence Bell opposed them as expensive to the State and an inducement to thriftlessness in early adult life. In essence the philosophy of *At the Works* is that less-adequate individuals may have to be guided towards the proper fulfilment of their responsibilities and that those who, through wealth and rank, are able to assist in this have a responsibility to do so. *At the Works* was intended to raise awareness of social issues among her own class. By 1908, besides her own group of lady visitors, Florence Bell was paying the salaries of three professional district visitors – in effect the region's first social workers. The function of visitors was not to distribute direct charity but to advise on housecraft and child welfare, thereby helping the wives and mothers of Teesside to fulfil their duties more completely.

She seems to have perceived *At the Works* as supplying what Rowntree and Booth could not as men ever provide: a frank assessment of society based on a female perspective of female roles. She could be scathing about the failings (as she saw them) of her sex whilst making observations about childbirth, miscarriage and the menopause which seem very 'modern' to readers today. Throughout, *At the Works* is distinguished by its author's empathy for those who managed, on a very limited means, the homes it describes and it is this quality – along with the wealth of evidence it contains – that has ensured continuing interest in the book.

Florence Bell herself was surprised by the success of *At the Works* and tentative about the 1911 publication of a cheap popular edition. In it, she wrote, the book had 'apparently made on the minds of many readers a more painful impression than I believe to be justified by the facts'. Concluding that the reissue might 'be read by many of those whose lives are described in its pages' and that 'it is their verdict that I shall value most of all', she was at pains to stress that 'so many men and women are steering their lives along a worthy and honourable course'. She was also aware that events were overtaking the book but, unlike Rowntree, never attempted to extend or update her research. The sole addition to the main text of the 1911 edition is a note about the Middlesbrough Winter Gardens, temperance coffee and entertainment rooms for workers and their families which she had been instrumental in opening.

After 1904, when her husband inherited Lowthian Bell's baronetcy and country seat at Rounton in the North Riding, Florence Bell spent much less time on Teesside; but she continued to write, publishing an edition of the letters of her step-daughter, the Islamicist and traveller Gertrude Bell, when she was 76. In the same year Sybil Thorndike produced Bell's last play, *Angela* in London. *Landmarks*, Florence Bell's final and in some ways most revealing book appeared just a year before she died. Family sources recall that massive bonfires were lit to consume her voluminous correspondence and papers after her death.

Bibliography

Florence Bell, *At the Works: A Study of a Manufacturing Town*, London, Nelson, 1907; second edition 1911; republished Newton Abbott, David & Charles, 1969, with an introduction by Frederick Alderson; London, Virago, 1985, with an introduction by Angela V. John, and Middlesbrough, Teesside University Press, 1997, with an introduction by Jim Turner.

Florence Bell, *Landmarks: A Reprint of Some Essays and Other Pieces Published between the Years 1894 and 1922*, London, Nelson, 1929.

Tony Donajgrodzki, 'An even vision: the ideology of 'At the Works'', *Bulletin of the Cleveland & Teesside Local History Society*, 55, 1988.

Tyne Tees Television, *At the Works*, (television documentary series 1987), with accompanying booklet with the same title by Pat Whaley and Malcolm Chase.

Malcolm Chase

John Hyslop Bell, (c.1833–1920) **Newspaper Founder and Coroner**

John Hyslop Bell was born in Dumfriesshire, Scotland about 1833. At the age of 18 he went to London to become a civil servant but three years later, he became a Parliamentary and Law correspondent. In 1855, he came north to join a newspaper in Sunderland which then merged with other papers to form the Liberal paper, the *South Durham and Cleveland Mercury*. Bell was editor and co-proprietor of this Hartlepool-based publication, and a Hartlepool town councillor. In 1869, as the leading newspaper man in the North East, he was invited to Darlington by the town's Liberal establishment to found *The Northern Echo* which he first published on 1 January 1870. At Bell's instigation, it was the country's first halfpenny daily newspaper.

J. H. Bell, Founder of *The Northern Echo*

In August 1871 he appointed W. T. Stead editor of the paper, an inspired step as Stead was just 22 and had no newspaper experience. Stead established the *Echo's* reputation as a campaigning newspaper locally, nationally and internationally. In 1874, under Bell and Stead's stewardship, the *Echo* was instrumental in returning the "Durham 13" to the House of Commons – all 13 of the county's MPs were Liberal for the first time in its history. Bell was the *Echo's* sole proprietor and from 1874, added the *Darlington and Stockton Times* and the *Darlington and Richmond Herald and Telegraph* to his stable. However, in 1889 he suddenly severed ties with the group's other directors after a disagreement over support for Irish Home Rule. He retired from newspapers and became a Justice of the Peace for the Cleveland area – he lived in Seaton Carew with his wife, Alice, and six children. In 1893, he toured India on behalf of the Purity Association, and in 1897 he became coroner for Stockton. In 1914 he conducted the inquests into the deaths of 138 people killed by bombardment from three German battle cruisers at the Hartlepools. He retired in 1919 and died on 5 May 1920, aged 88 at his home of St Fillians, Stockton. His obituary in the *Darlington and Stockton Times* said he was "a brilliant, experienced and enterprising newspaperman ... the *Echo* in his hands did splendid work for the (Liberal) party and its achievements acquired a fame far beyond its local limits". He is buried in West Cemetery, Darlington.

Bibliography

Chris Lloyd, *Attacking the Devil: 130 Years of The Northern Echo*, The *Northern Echo*, 1999.

Chris Lloyd

John Butterfield (1865–1939)   J.P., Hospital Administrator

When John Butterfield died in February 1939 following a tragic accident as he was boarding a tramcar, the newspaper report recorded him as being one of the best known and respected men on Wearside.

He was born in Durham in 1865, the son of a railway worker who had moved from Barnard Castle and, at the age of 16, he was working as a printer and stationer, and living with his parents, two sisters and a brother. Having gained experience in Durham and, for a short while in Newcastle, in 1884 he moved to Sunderland to be a compositor on the old *Sunderland Daily Post*. Here he had experience of the editorial and commercial branches, and was also in charge of the advertising department.

In 1888 he married Dorothy Wilson, the eldest daughter of John Wilson, the Durham miners' leader. The marriage took place in the Jubilee

Methodist Chapel, North Road, Durham, and they made their home in Sunderland. Here they became members of Williamson Terrace Methodist Chapel and, for fifty years, their work for the Church became a leading interest in their lives.

It was in 1899 that John became involved in politics when he was appointed Secretary and Registration Agent to the Sunderland Liberal Association. He held this position for nearly twenty years and, in addition to being responsible for several successful election campaigns, he assisted in almost every by-election in the North-East. In 1915 he became a Councillor for Colliery Ward in Sunderland, and held this seat for seven years. Congratulations on this achievement came not only from his many supporters, but also from friends with opposing views. During the war years he took on additional voluntary service as a Special Constable.

John Butterfield, from a photograph supplied by Brenda White

At the end of the war, in 1918, John Butterfield was appointed Secretary of Durham County and Sunderland Eye Infirmary, and the work of maintaining this growing hospital by voluntary contributions became his main aim. Through his collections he gained a great knowledge of the town and, it was said, he could direct anyone by the churches or the public houses – although he was a teetotaller! The hospital already had a great reputation for eye surgery, but its premises were much too small for further expansion. Support was gained from local industries such as mining and ship-building and he was involved in persuading local personalities to further the funding of a new hospital. Eventually a new site was obtained and planning began. One of the generous benefactors was Sir John Priestman, and it was decided to name the new building the Sir John Priestman Durham County and Sunderland Eye Infirmary.

John Butterfield's many appointments reflected his love and care for those in need and, for thirty years, he was on the Board of Guardians for the Poor Law Institute and on two occasions was chairman, or "Father" of the Board. After the passing of the Board in 1930, he was a member of the Sunderland Public Assistance Committee for the first few years of its existence. For several years he was also chairman of the Rate and Rent Payers' Association.

In 1933, John Butterfield's position as a respected and trusted figure in the town was recognised when he was made a magistrate for the county borough of Sunderland.

Through all the developments in his working life, he continued to be active in his church work. For 48 years he was secretary of the Church Trust, and was Superintendent of the Sunday School for 25 years. The extent of his influence on the children in the area will never be known, but many acknowledged the effect of his guidance. As secretary of the Primitive Methodist Circuit, he was a delegate to the Uniting Conference of Methodism in London in September 1932. He then became secretary of the Sunderland North Circuit of churches.

On 4 February 1939, at an age when many men would be enjoying retirement, John Butterfield was returning to the "Eye Infirmary" after lunch when he was involved in an accident as he was boarding a tramcar on Roker Promenade – a few yards from his home. This led to his death a few days later. At the inquest, a verdict was returned of "Accidental death with no blame attached to anyone". Later it was disclosed that while he was lying waiting for the ambulance, his thoughts were not for his own condition but for others, as he told the driver and conductor not to worry, as he would see they did not get into trouble for the accident. The Coroner said "I feel I have lost a sincere friend, while the town has lost an excellent citizen, and the community one who laboured willingly and long to serve his fellow men."

His death, so soon after he and his wife Dorothy celebrated their Golden Wedding, was a great sadness to his family of one son and three daughters. At his funeral they were joined by many representatives from the activities with which he had been connected.

Footnote. The "Sir John Priestman Durham County and Sunderland Eye Infirmary" removed to Queen Alexandra Road in 1940 and was ultimately taken into the Health Service in 1948. Williamson Terrace Methodist Chapel was destroyed by bombs in April 1943.

Bibliography

Newspaper reports, *The Northern Echo, Sunderland Echo, Sunderland Gazette*, February 1939.

William Robinson, M.S., M.D., D.Ch., F.R.C.S., *Centenary 1836–1936 of the Durham County and Sunderland Eye Infirmary*, Printed by Robert Youll, 1936.

The 1881 Census.

Brenda P. White

Augusta Ada Byron, Countess Lovelace (1815–1852)   Mathematician

When Anna Isabella Milbanke married George Gordon Noel Byron (Lord Byron) in Seaham Hall on 2 January 1815 there were those who said there was no chance of a successful marriage, because it had not taken place in the neighbouring Saxon church. Their predictions were fulfilled when the couple separated just over a year later and this was closely followed by Byron's self-imposed exile.

Although their time together was so short the marriage was consummated and on 10 December 1815 Lady Byron was delivered of a girl, Augusta Ada Byron. Her father saw his daughter only during the first weeks of her life. She remained with her mother who enthused her with her own passion for mathematics. Women were not at that time permitted to enrol for a university education and Ada was obliged to follow her own course of study. As her ideas developed she was introduced to Mary Somerville, a mathematician, who encouraged her to continue her studies. She in turn introduced Ada to other mathematicians and also to William Lord King who, although several years older, became her husband in 1835 when she was just nineteen.

There were three children from their marriage, respectively in 1836 (Byron Noel), 1837 (Anne Isabella) and 1839 (Ralph Gordon).

William King, who became the Earl of Lovelace in 1838, encouraged her in her studies, mainly under the tutelage of Augustus de Morgan (1806–1871). In 1827 de Morgan was appointed to the chair of mathematics in the newly founded University College, London.

Augusta Ada Byron, Countess Lovelace, portrait downloaded from WWW

Over a period of eighteen years from 1836 Ada communicated regularly with Charles Babbage and it was this relationship which was to bring her to the notice of mathematicians. Babbage was co-founder of the Analytical Society in 1820 and in 1831 he helped to found the British Association for the Advancement of Science. He is credited with the design

26

of the first computer, his Analytical Machine. He was supported by government funds which were eventually withdrawn before the project was completed. It was with this project that Ada, Countess Lovelace, was involved.

Babbage was not the best of communicators and was unable to explain the theory behind his idea. In 1842 the Italian Ambassador to France, L. F. Menebrea, delivered a lecture in French explaining the theory. Subsequently Ada translated the paper into English and added her own notes which substantially extended the paper. This she could only have done as a result of understanding the theories expounded. She provided an example of how the machine could be used to compute Bernoulli numbers. Unfortunately it was considered inappropriate for a lady, especially of the upper class, to publish such a serious study. Consequently she signed the work "A.A.L".

Unfortunately Ada's relationship with Babbage resulted in an even less successful project. Their mathematical interests were used in studies of the theory of probability in horse racing. Instead of relieving Babbage of his financial problems his debts were compounded. Worse was to befall Lady Lovelace who had to pawn the family jewels to pay off her creditors.

She died of cancer in 1852 and is buried alongside her father.

Although not given the recognition of which she was worthy during her life her contribution to the history of computing is now well rewarded. She is recognised by many, although not all, as the first computer programmer. In 1970 the American Department of Defense introduced a new computer programming language. This they named the Ada language.

Bibliography

Doris Langley Moore, *Ada, Countess of Lovelace, Byron's legitimate daughter*, John Murray, London, 1977.

Searching the Internet using the following keywords will proffer a considerable amount of information: Ada; "Ada King"; "Ada Lovelace"; "Charles Babbage".

Dorothy Stein, *Ada, A Life and a Legacy*, MIT, Mass, 1984.

Betty Alexandra Toole, *Ada, The Enchantress of Numbers*, Strawberry Press, 1998.

Donald Miller

John Alan Chalmers (1904–1967)   Physicist and Durham Scout Leader

S on of Stephen (born in Australia) and Clara (née Rosenhain) John Alan Chalmers was born at Hornsey, Middlesex, on 29 September 1904. His father was a Lecturer in Optics. He joined the 66th North London Group of Scouts as a Rover and took part in its Summer Camp at Clacton (1921). At the University of Cambridge he studied physics and graduated in 1926 with a first-class degree. Afterwards he did research, working under the distinguished scientist, Ernest, Lord Rutherford. At the same time he was Assistant Scout Master of the 10th Cambridge Scouts and went to camp with them in England and Switzerland.

J. A. Chalmers, Glencoe trip, 1965 (D/SG 6/46)

In 1928 Chalmers came as Lecturer to the developing Physics Department at Durham University. Two years later he was awarded the Cambridge Ph.D. degree for his research at the Cavendish Laboratory on radioactivity.

Chalmers' 'brains carried him to science, his heart to Scouting'. He started the 5th Durham (St. Mary-le-Bow) Group on 22 November 1928, the first six scouts being choirboys of that church. By the end of the year the number had increased to 16. In September 1930 a 'Den' was obtained in Back Silver Street. The link with the church was severed in 1936 and the Group became 'Open'. Chalmers was always known to his boys as 'Skip' – his personal preference. Everyone in Durham knew who Skip Chalmers was. He kept meticulous Log Books, full of amusing accounts of meetings, camps, concerts and money-raising events, all illustrated with photographs (mostly taken by himself). In 1938 he wrote a short 'History of 10 Years' for the Log, giving details of boys passing tests, gaining Proficiency Badges and winning Cups; the starting of a Cub Pack in 1929, also a Rover Crew in 1933; and noting that 'the Scout Master has had assistance from many helpers' (DRO, D/SG 4/5).

Dr. Chalmers' days were spent at the University Science Laboratories or associated sites. In 1932 his chosen field of interest was atmospheric electricity (lightning) and he pursued this enthusiastically for the rest of his life. He had various scientific devices in huts between the laboratories and Little High Wood for the purpose of measuring the electrical properties of the atmosphere. In addition he fixed detectors and equipment high in the Pennines. He and his research students worked together and the results were published in some hundred scientific papers. He also wrote two books on atmospheric electricity (1949 and 1957). Through these publications he became an international authority and many foreign students came to learn from him.

Skip had a large open-topped car, often with a trailer attached, which he used to transport the scouts. Photographs of it during the 1939–45 war show the boys collecting unneeded books for the war effort. It was replaced by a van bought expressly for use with the scouts. Skip became an Assistant County Commissioner (for Relationships) on 28 May 1941 and was awarded the Scout Medal of Merit in 1942. After the war, he took members of the 5th Durhams abroad to Scout Jamborees. About ten would go in a minibus and sight-seeing was included. At the 7th World Rover Moot in Australia (1961–62) he met some of his relatives there and they helped him to compile his family tree. Because of his experience of scouting in other countries he was asked to be Assistant County Commissioner (International) from 21

November 1962. His travels and correspondence enabled him to make a fine collection of foreign stamps, also of scout flags and badges.

Birthday parties were held for the 21st (1949), 25th (1953) and 35th (1963) anniversaries of the flourishing 5th Durham. These were all jolly occasions for past and present members, parents and senior Scouting Officers, finishing with songs around the camp fire. At the first of these events the County Commissioner (the tenth Lord Barnard) presented Skip with a bar to his Medal of Merit; and, at the second, Skip received a carved oak book-case which was handed over by one of the original six scouts, on behalf of the Group.

In 1947 Dr Chalmers had been promoted to Senior Lecturer and in 1957 he was made Reader. Following a grant from the U.S. Navy in 1963 he said, 'It may appear fantastic but we are hoping our research ... may one day be able to achieve this' [i.e. the taming of lightning]. 'If we can, we will then be able to prevent the vast amount of damage caused by lightning ... Durham [is] the leading centre in Britain in the subject' (DRO, D/SG 6/44). Dr. Chalmers also acted as consultant for the Admiralty and the U.S. Air Force. The BBC and ITV invited him to appear on television. With his fees he took the six Patrol Leaders on a climbing holiday in Scotland the following year. In October 1965 he was appointed to a Personal Professorship in Physics.

On 24 August 1966 Skip undertook the duties of District Commissioner for Durham City. He was planning to take a party of scouts to the World Jamboree in Idaho, U.S.A., a year later. He himself never got there because he became unwell and, after a two-months' illness, he died on 14 March 1967.

The unexpected death of this well-loved and active man shocked and grieved all who knew him. At his funeral in St. Margaret's church 'the black-gowned dignitaries of the University and the picturesque Boy Scouts and Rovers ... demonstrated that [he] had performed the extraordinary feat of living two lives at once ... [This] was possible only to a rare and astonishing person; he was, indeed, unique'. Scouts and their parents, as well as colleagues, remember him with respect and affection. Perhaps one Senior Scout, writing in the Log Book on 15 December 1962, may express the feelings of all scouts: 'Thanks a lot, Skip, for a holiday I will never forget and for putting up with me for so long. I know your main interest is our welfare and I am sure that you will be fully rewarded for it' (DRO, D/SG 6/42).

The Silver Acorn Medal, the second highest award in Scouting, was awarded posthumously to Skip on 23 April 1967, 'for services of exceptional character' (given to the 5th Durham Scouts for safe-keeping).

Bibliography

Durham County Advertiser, 17 and 24 March 1967.

Information from Mr. J. Lowerson (secretary, Durham Scout County), Mr. K. Robertson (Group Scout Leader, 5th Durham City Scout Group) and Sir Arnold Wolfendale, F.R.S. (Department of Physics, University of Durham).

Papers of 5th Durham Scouts at Durham Record Office (DRO, D/SG), deposited by the Group Scout Leader.

University of Durham Gazette, Vol. XII (New Series) No. 3 (26 June 1965), and Vol. XIV (New Series) No. 2 (31 March 1967).

Dorothy M. Meade

Frederick Maddick Dawson OBE (1912–1988)   Local Government

Fred Dawson spent all his working life in the North East, beginning at 16 as a Junior Council Clerk at Tynemouth. He is best remembered for his work after the Second World War as Clerk to Billingham Urban District Council during its development as a New Town in all but name and subsequently as Director of the North East Development Council.

Dawson was appointed Clerk to Billingham UDC in 1947, and during his 20 years' service there Billingham changed from a little known place to a large, thriving and progressive town. With an enthusiastic council he oversaw this transformation. So great was his impact that he was dubbed 'Mr Billingham' and the new town centre 'Dawson City'. He earned a formidable reputation for energy, efficiency and creativity, and for cutting through red tape.

Harry Davies, a Stockton councillor who served with Dawson, paid tribute to 'this remarkable man': 'Fred Dawson was a man of tremendous energy and vision. He did things which were thought impossible and always found loopholes. He was a dynamo. But behind his facade as a ruthless organiser and motivator, he was a gentle, caring person.' (*Evening Gazette* obituary, 2 December 1988.)

Billingham UDC had been formed in 1923, following the formation of the fertiliser plant of Synthetic Ammonia and Nitrates Ltd., later to become ICI. Billingham and ICI expanded together, the town development underpinned by industrial rates. Model housing in Mill Lane and Roscoe Road by ICI for its workforce was followed in the 1920s and 1930s by UDC garden city housing around Chilton Lane, Belasis Lane, High Clarence, Cowpen Lane and Central Avenue. After the Second World War, expansion moved northwards towards and beyond the designated site of the new town centre.

F. M. Dawson, from a photograph supplied by Vera Chapman courtesy of Ailsa M. H. Dick

During Dawson's stewardship, Billingham was a place where everything seemed possible. The Dawson era was the boom era. The new town centre was begun in early 1950, and was developed further from 1958 around pedestrianised squares. The Kennedy Gardens flats were built in 1962 and the Forum sports and leisure centre was completed in 1967, shortly before Dawson's retirement. The whole town centre was supplied by a NCB block heating system for which it was awarded the NALGO Accolade for Enterprise in 1966. Billingham had now pioneered the country's first District Heating Scheme, first combined Sports and Leisure Centre and first College of Further Education.

In October 1967, H. M. Queen Elizabeth II accompanied by His Royal Highness the Prince Philip, after opening the Tyne Tunnel, travelled by train to Billingham. Here they unveiled in the East Precinct the Family Group statue by Bainbridge Copnall which represents the spirit of the town. They opened and toured the Forum, then continued to Darlington for its Borough Centenary celebrations.

In 1968, however, under Local Government Reorganisation, the County Borough of Teesside was formed and Billingham lost its independence. By this time, Fred Dawson had been appointed Director of the North East Development Council. The *Northern Echo* pointed out that Dawson's 'reputation for cutting through red tape should be valuable at the Development Council, for one of his chief tasks is to kick and shout'. Being an unofficial body, it could be more vocal than official bodies. Its role as a pressure group to put forward the claims and attractions of the North East for industrial development was already beginning to transform the region. Having taken over from George Chetwynd, Dawson served from 1967 until 1972. On retirement he was awarded the OBE for his services to the community.

In 1981, Fred became the Chairman of the Special Programmes Board of the new County Durham Manpower Services Commission made up of representatives of industry, commerce, trade unions, local authorities, voluntary bodies and other interested groups to spearhead the MSC's youth opportunities campaign in the North.

He died at his Darlington home in 1988.

Bibliography

Vera Chapman, *Around Billingham*, The Chalford Publishing Co. Ltd., 1996.

Evening Gazette, 2 December 1988.

Northern Echo, 20 October 1967.

Northern Echo, 3 November 1988.

Francis Gerard Owens, *Billingham from Earliest Times to the Modern Day*, 1995.

Vera Chapman

Charles Dickens (1812–1870)   Novelist

Charles Dickens first visited Durham county in 1838. On 31 January he stayed overnight at the George Inn at Greta Bridge (at that time in Yorkshire) and next morning travelled by post-chaise to Barnard Castle where he stayed for two nights at the King's Head (now the Dickens Coffee Shoppe) in the Market Place. He was accompanied by his illustrator, Hablot Knight Browne ('Phiz'), and their object was to gather information about the 'Yorkshire Schools' which would provide the major satirical theme of *Nicholas Nickleby*. Barnard Castle became 'the market town' of the novel, and Newman Noggs specifically names the town when he recommends the ale at the King's Head (Chapter 6); the retired farmer, John Browdie, goes to live in the town (Chapter 64) apparently in a house in Galgate. Dickens was helped in his enquiries by a local solicitor, Richard Barnes, and a Mr McKay who ran a school at the lower end of The Bank, after he had been discharged from the staff of William Shaw's Academy at Bowes; Dickens visited the Academy, which is generally accepted as the original of 'Dotheboys Hall' in the novel, and met Mr. Shaw.

The publication of *Nicholas Nickleby* was, at least in part, responsible for the closure of the 'Yorkshire Schools'. This had a considerable impact on the economy of Teesdale, for a significant number of employees at the schools, including cooks, sempstresses, and cleaners as well as teachers, became unemployed. Furthermore, frugally as the pupils were fed, food suppliers also keenly felt the loss of trade and for many years Dickens was regarded with much disfavour by residents in the area, particularly in the market town of Barnard Castle.

While in Barnard Castle, Dickens noted the shop of Thomas Humphreys, clockmaker, which stood at Amen Corner (now a small rose-garden near the parish church) and used his name, minus the 's', in the title of *Master Humphrey's Clock* in 1840. Barnard Castle also became 'the market town' in *The Holly-Tree* (1855). Dickens went from Barnard Castle to Darlington to catch the York coach. While waiting, he read an article about himself in *The Durham Advertiser*, and wrote a sharp letter to the editor, pointing out errors in the article.

Dickens revisited Darlington during his reading tour of 1861 and his performance was so well received that he commented, 'Little Darlington covered itself in glory.' He had a sad association with Darlington when his only surviving brother, Fred, died there in 1868; he had lodged in Elton Parade while working as a journalist, and his grave is in the West Cemetery.

Oil painting by Daniel MacLise, 1839, Tate Gallery

Durham City provided a 'capital' audience for Dickens' readings and he visited Sunderland twice. He managed, directed, wrote and acted for the Amateur Players and in 1852 the company presented a bill of three plays at the newly-built Lyceum in Lambton Street, Sunderland. It was an unnerving experience, for the ceiling lights swayed during outbreaks of loud applause and Dickens feared that the audience might stampede for safety. Always busy during tours, Dickens nevertheless found time to take the waters at Shotley Spa. During the 1861 tour he gave a reading in the Music Hall in Wilson Street, Sunderland.

Dickens' last associations with the county were posthumous. During World War II items from the Dickens House museum in London were widely distributed throughout the country. About fifty items were kept in the strong-room of Barnard Castle Urban District Council Offices; they included manuscript pages and printed instalments of *Nicholas Nickleby* and a lock of Dickens' hair.

Postscript: In 1988 Barnard Castle celebrated the 150th anniversary of Dickens' visit. The novelist's great-great-grandson, Mr Christopher Dickens, repeated in a stage-coach his ancestor's journey from Greta Bridge to Barnard Castle and, later, to Bowes where, outside 'Dotheboys Hall', he met Mr Edwin Shaw, the great-great-grandson of William Shaw, the schoolmaster whom Charles Dickens had met there in 1838.

Bibliography

Peter Ackroyd, *Dickens*, 1990.

J. E. Buckrose, *Rambles in the Yorkshire Dales*, 1913.

T. P. Cooper, *With Dickens in Yorkshire*, 1923.

Una Pope-Hennessy, *Charles Dickens*, 1945.

Alan Wilkinson

Charles Duncan (1865–1933)   **M.P. and trade unionist**

Charles Duncan, Labour M.P. and trade union leader, was born on 8 June 1865 at his parents' home, 93 Stockton Street, Middlesbrough. His father was a Tees River pilot. Charles was educated at the Middlesbrough National School where, he later said, he was 'distinguished chiefly for his fighting propensities'. Yet Duncan, helped by his father's ability to pay, remained in full-time education until sixteen and throughout his life showed a marked bookish inclination. 'I am a very wide reader – all is fish that comes into my net; and I like to buy books ... I am rather proud of my collection, as it represents practically *all my spare cash as well as my taste in literature*.' Duncan claimed that the authors who had most influenced him were Carlyle, Ruskin, Plato and the American environmentalist Henry Thoreau. He joined the local temperance movement (notable for its radical politics ever since Chartism, James Maw and John Kane, q.q.v.) at an early age and was a lifelong teetotaller, always remembering, as he put it, 'the misery and degradation caused by drink' on Teesside.

Duncan was not inclined to follow his father's career, even though recruitment to the pilotage was hereditary. After a short spell in coastal shipping, spent with a view to becoming a ship's engineer, Duncan returned to Middlesbrough and an apprenticeship at the Teesside Iron and Engine Works. On completing his time he worked briefly at Elswick ordnance factory on Tyneside. Here he joined the Amalgamated Society of Engineers (ASE) and, a convert to socialism, the Independent Labour Party (ILP). Back in Middlesbrough he became one of the town's earliest and most enthusiastic ILP-ers, coming to the public eye as one of the organisers of a soup kitchen in Middlesbrough for the unemployed during the winter of 1891. Soon afterwards, he was elected to the local Board of Poor Law Guardians and, in 1895, to the Corporation. ILP councillors were regarded with some suspicion and in Duncan's case it is not hard to see why. Duncan was secretary of the local branch of the recently formed Workers' Union (WU) which had a high profile in the town. He became a full-time official in 1898, the same year that he secured a minimum weekly wage for Council employees of 21 shillings (a relatively high sum for unskilled manual workers). In 1900, encouraged by Duncan in seeking to enforce a 'closed shop', WU members employed by the Corporation went on strike. They were defeated and dismissed from their jobs. Under something of a cloud, Duncan did not seek re-election; but he was clearly ambitious and may have already known that he would shortly leave Teesside. He had already risen to become national president of the WU and, from the close of 1900, was its General Secretary, based in London.

His ties with the North-East were now tenuous. Duncan succeeded in making both the WU and himself significant forces in British industry and by 1914 WU membership stood at 140,000. Elected M.P. for Barrow-in-Furness in 1906, Duncan was part of the first parliamentary Labour Party. He sat for Barrow until 1918 and for Clay Cross, Derbyshire, from 1922 until his death. In politics his innate moderation was more apparent than it had been as a union organiser. During the First World War he was a leading supporter of the British Workers' League, a nationalistic pro-war body. He served on various official committees directing labour supply into the war effort and was sent by Lloyd George to America to campaign for its entry into the war. The post-war phase of Duncan's career was not, however, distinguished. After various vicissitudes the WU was absorbed into the Transport and General Workers' Union in 1929. As an M.P. Duncan was guaranteed a place in the union's inner circle right up to his death. However, the career of the charismatic Middlesbrough engineer and visionary of general unionism ended on a decidedly muted note, chiefly remembered as 'the best dressed man in the House of Commons'.

Bibliography

C. Duncan, 'How I got on', *Pearson's Weekly*, 15 February 1906.

D. Howell, *British Workers and the Independent Labour Party, 1888–1906*, Manchester University Press, 1983.

R. Hyman, *The Workers' Union*, Oxford University Press, 1971.

D. E. Martin, 'Charles Duncan', in J. Bellamy and J. Saville (eds), *Dictionary of Labour Biography*, vol. 2, London, Macmillan, 1974, 123–27.

Malcolm Chase

William Falla II (1761–1830)   Nurseryman

William Falla II took over his father's thriving nursery in Gateshead in 1804. The nursery was previously owned by George Dale (1705–1781). William Falla I embarked upon his career with William Joyce (d.1767), a competitor of George Dale. Joyce was a successful nurseryman who also advised on landscape design. He was particularly favoured by the local gentry such as George Bowes at Gibside and Joseph Spence, prebendary at Durham 1754. In 1810 William Falla II disposed of his father's nursery at Hebburn and established a tree nursery on land which was formerly part of Felling Hall Estate.

William Falla II's shrewd expansion of the forest tree nursery enabled him to sell large quantities of stock cheaply to local entrepreneurs who were developing commercial forest plantations of oak, elm, beech and larch and planting enclosure hedges. By 1813 William Falla II was commissioned to plant 900 acres of woodland at Chopwell, Gateshead, restocked Levens Hall in Cumbria and supplied the Marquis of Londonderry at Wynyard Hall, County Durham. Falla's large scale operations required new technology and in 1816 he was experimenting with ploughs and drilling equipment. He capitalised on both supplying and planting and employed gangs of local men. Whilst under the management of William Falla II the nursery was reputedly the largest in Britain.

A catalogue published by the firm in 1797 ran to 35 pages. By 1827 it amounted to 64 pages offering a staggering 415 varieties of fruit trees. William Falla II was a founding member of the Botanical and Horticultural Society of Durham, Northumberland and Newcastle upon Tyne, a society which held regular meetings to exhibit fruit, flowers and garden vegetables.

He was a well respected member of local society and died in August 1830. William Falla III did not inherit his father's business acumen and within six years of taking over one of the most successful nurseries in Britain he became bankrupt and disappeared. A month later his body was found in Ravensworth Woods where he had committed suicide.

Bibliography

Durham County Record Office, Salvin Papers.

John Harvey, *Early Gardening Catalogues*, Phillimore, 1972.

John Harvey, *Early Nurserymen*, Phillimore, 1974.

John Harvey, 'Prices of Trees and Shrubs 1754', *Garden History*, vol. 2 (2), 34, 44, 1974.

Map of Newcastle and Gateshead engraved by L. A. Kidd, 1802.

1855 edition Ordnance Survey 25" scale Sheet IV.

Newcastle Magazine, vol. 1, p. 514, 1820.

Oxberry Papers, Gateshead Library.

Fiona Green

William George Footitt (1865–1936)   **Architectural Draughtsman**

The son of Martin and Adelaide (née Holmes) Footitt, William George Footitt was born in Lincoln on 17 October 1865. His father was a waterman. By the age of 15, still in Lincoln, he was working as an 'architect's pupil' (1881 Census). A small drawing by him survives of an 'Old House on E side of Trent – Gainsbro'. He recorded that it was 'Inked in' (2 August 1888) and 'Sketched some time ago (while 'Argo' was 'driving' thro' 'Roads') – from cog-boat' (Footitt Papers, 'Decoration', Dean and Chapter Library, Durham).

It would seem that he came to the attention of the Durham architect, Charles Hodgson Fowler, who did a lot of work in Lincolnshire and who had family connections there. Mr Fowler offered the young man a post in his Durham firm (47, North Bailey) and , by the Census of April 1891, the 'architect's assistant' was boarding at 36, Hallgarth Street. However, he had been in Durham since at least Whit Monday (10 June) 1889, when he sketched details of the church porch at Brancepeth. (Footitt Papers, Print

393 i). His skills were soon recognised and used. During an account of the AGM (1893) in the *Trans. D&N.* IV, 1890–95 (1896) he was referred to as 'a gentleman in Mr Fowler's office, who had made the very accurate drawings of the crosses' [which had been found in the Chapter House restoration].

On 5 June 1895 Footitt married Christina Ross, daughter of Donald Ross, a forester, in Lincoln. They lived in 16, Providence Row, where a son, John Martin, was born on 11 May 1896. The family attended St. Nicholas' church.

St. Oswald's Schools, Durham, from a photograph
in the collection of M. F. Richardson

Canon Joseph Thomas Fowler wrote many articles on lesser-known places and objects in the north of England. Some of those in Durham City were illustrated by Footitt: part of the cloister ceiling (east side) re cathedral fireplace (*Proc. S.A.L.* 2nd ser. XIX (1901–03)); monumental effigy near the cathedral north door in *Trans. D&N.* VI Pt. 2, 1906–11 (1912); plans and elevations of gatehouse of Durham Abbey (*Trans.* as above) – 'The drawings for these have been prepared with great care by Mr W. G. Footitt, whose name is a sufficient warrant for their perfect accuracy.' The plan of medieval Durham, drawn to illustrate *The Rites of Durham* (ed. J. T. Fowler, SS 107, 1902), is almost certainly by Footitt.

In 1899 *A Catalogue of the Sculptured and Inscribed Stones in the Cathedral Library, Durham* was published, the Anglian stones being described by Dr. William Greenwell. The preface by Dean G. W. Kitchin refers to 'Mr W. G. Footitt, who has enriched the Catalogue with a large number of most accurate drawings, in which the characteristic work of the original is admirably represented'. A reviewer in *The Durham Chronicle* (18 August 1899) writes about Footitt as 'our able and artistic townsman', a gratifying compliment to one not born in the city.

A description of St Cuthbert's coffin (following Greenwell's study of the pieces) was added to the *Catalogue*, illustrated 'by the excellent drawings made by the skilful and appreciative hand of Mr. Footitt'. This was the first reconstruction on paper of the coffin. (It was superseded in 1950 by the drawings of Donald McIntyre in *The Coffin of Saint Cuthbert*.) Before the book was published the grave of St Cuthbert had been re-opened. Some more fragments of the coffin were recovered and inserted into Greenwell's arrangement, 'a valuable piece of work due to the keen eye and patient labour of Mr. Footitt'. At the same time the skeleton of St Cuthbert and the head of St Oswald were temporarily removed. These were examined by Dr Selby W. Plummer and the two skulls were drawn by Footitt (W. Brown and S. W. Plummer, *St. Cuthbert's Remains*, 1899).

In 1912 Dean Kitchin wrote *The Story of the Deanery, Durham*. His preface states: 'And the pencil of Mr. Footitt, as graceful as it is unerring, ever helps the interpretation of the true look of the house, so hard to be given by mere word-painting.'

Footitt's interest in his adopted city produced several drawings in his careful, architectural style: the decaying mansion house at Kepier in 1890; a drawing of Church Street (3 June 1891), showing St Oswald's Schools; the Jesuits' Chapel and Residence at 44 and 45, Old Elvet (1899), from *The Story of an Old Mission*, by William Brown (the last three being from the collection of M. F. Richardson); a plan of Durham in Caldcleugh's *Popular Guide to the City of Durham, Cathedral and Castle* (1906), printed in many subsequent editions; fine ink drawings of St Nicholas' church and the cathedral in one particular book (6 June 1906) in private possession. This was presented to the Revd. C. Wright, curate, on his leaving the parish. It accompanied a gold watch, given by the St Nicholas' Men's Service (of which Footitt was a member) and other church groups; preliminary drawing of St Margaret's church hall, c. 1912 (collection of M. F. Richardson); Kepier farmhouse (June 1917) and also a plan of the mansion house ruin (September 1917), both in Gibby Negatives Collection, Durham University Library, DUL K13 and K14b, respectively; and three small notebooks, covering the years 1908–22, presented to the Dean and Chapter Library, the first and third by Dean J. E. C. Welldon and J. Meade Faulkner, respectively (Hunter MSS 145–7): they include drawings of the arms of the Bishops of Durham, arms on some bosses of the cloister ceiling, certain memorial stones in St Giles' churchyard and the shield ('practically obliterated') in the Pineapple wall, Old Durham.

When C. Hodgson Fowler died in 1910, Footitt, his principal draughtsman, accompanied the family mourners to Nettleham, near Lincoln, for the burial. He probably carried with him a brass altar cross, designed by Fowler himself (Footitt Papers, 'Emblems') for presentation to the church (missing after 1969).

After the First World War Footitt was asked to design his parish War Memorial, a large, alabaster mural tablet which can still be seen in St Nicholas' church. This was unveiled on 14 May 1922.

Footitt continued to work in the firm, now taken over by W. H. Wood. His wife died on 6 March 1924. On 9 August 1929 his son, then teaching in Blackpool, married Elizabeth Shipley in Newcastle. Footitt died on 20 November 1936 and would have been buried beside his wife in St Nicholas' churchyard (although no memorial stone has been found). Unusual reminders of him – a little bit of fun on his part – are the several small mosaic tiles he inserted in the east wall of No. 16 The College, then the home of C. Hodgson Fowler (Mr. Martin Snape, from information given by the late Mr. Joseph Higgins, of the cathedral staff). An extract from a letter written in 1908 by Dr. Henry Gee, Master of University College, may serve to express the widespread esteem in which he was held: 'The work is excellent.... We are lucky to have you in Durham.' (Footitt Papers, 'Decoration').

Bibliography

W. Brown and S. W. Plummer, *St. Cuthbert's Remains*, 1899.

Thomas Caldcleugh and Son, *Popular Guide to the City of Durham, Cathedral and Castle*, 1906.

Footitt Papers and Hunter MSS in Dean and Chapter Library, Durham.

J. T. Fowler, (ed.), *The Rites of Durham*, 1902.

Gibby Negatives Collection, Durham University Library.

Dr. W. Greenwell, *A Catalogue of the Sculptured and Inscribed Stones in the Cathedral Library, Durham*, 1899.

Dr G. W. Kitchin, *The Story of the Deanery, Durham*, 1912.

D. McIntyre, and E. Kitzinger, *The Coffin of Saint Cuthbert*, 1950.

Transactions of the Architectural and Archaeological Society of Durham and Northumberland, Vol. IV, 1890–95 (1896); Vol. VI, Pt. 2, 1906–11 (1912).

Proc. S.A.L. 2nd ser. XIX (1901–03).

The Durham Chronicle, 18 August 1899.

Dorothy Meade

Samuel Galbraith J.P., O.B.E. (1853–1936)   Union Official and M.P.

Samuel Galbraith was born on 4 July 1853 in Ring Neil, Co. Down, Ireland. His father migrated to County Durham to work as a mason on the Marquis of Londonderry's estate at Wynyard Park. At the age of 10, he became a trapper at Trimdon Colliery and there rose at the face to become a hewer. He told the House of Commons in 1916 that his wages during the coal famine of the Franco–Prussian War (1870–71) were £5, £6 and £7 a week. His early life conformed to the pattern of youthful insouciance suddenly transformed by religion, which was the experience too of miners' leaders such as John Wilson and Peter Lee. After playing in a cricket match and spending the rest of the day in a pub until closing time, he experienced conversion at precisely 11.20 p.m. on Tuesday 25 August 1874. He turned against drink and sport. He joined the Methodist New Connexion. He learnt to read and write by attending Brandon village school, sitting among the junior and infant pupils. He thereafter read the Holy Bible from cover to cover every year for the rest of his life, and read the New Testament twice a year.

In 1879 he was elected checkweighman for Browney colliery. Through attendance at University Extension and evening lectures he obtained a mine manager's certificate in 1884 but he refused offers of managerial positions with mining companies. In 1885 he married Helen King Petty, a pupil teacher. In 1885 he was nominated for the Mid-Durham constituency but stood down in favour of John Wilson. In the same year, he was elected to Brandon Local Board and he continued as a member when it became the urban district for Brandon and Byshottles in 1895. In 1888 he was one of the miners' representatives elected to the first Durham county council. From

1894 to 1925 he was an alderman of Durham County Council. He became a justice of the peace in 1907. Throughout this period he was active in the Durham Miners' Association and in 1900 became one of the agents of the association and its general treasurer. He was a delegate to almost all the miners' international conferences down to 1914. Of the last, in Austria–Hungary, he told the Commons in 1919, 'I have never trusted Germans'. He loyally and vigorously supported the leadership of the DMA general secretaries, Crawford, Patterson and Wilson. He agreed with their emphasis upon executive control of the union and shared their distrust of lodge independence. They believed the survival and finances of the DMA depended upon co-operation, not confrontation, with employers. Strikes, he told the House of Commons in 1919, "breed mischief and create misery".

Samuel Galbraith, 1898

He succeeded John Wilson on his death as Liberal M.P. for Mid-Durham in 1915, in an unopposed return under the wartime party truce which was preceded by a struggle within the DMA Alderman W. House was first nominated by the union, in an attempt to have Wilson succeeded by a

44

Labour Party candidate. However, Galbraith put himself forward as the Liberal candidate. The Labour Party supporters claimed that the wartime truce only required that the traditional control of the seat by the miners be upheld. It was the national executive of the Labour Party which ruled that the strict interpretation of the truce called for a Liberal to continue to hold the seat. Had House taken the seat, he could have continued in his union office because a recent DMA change of rules allowed Labour M.P.s to retain union posts. Galbraith as a Liberal had of course to resign his union post. He was re-elected in 1918 for what was now the Spennymoor constituency, when he beat off a Labour Party challenge at the polls.

In his seven years in parliament, he spoke in only ten debates, five of which were concerned with the coal industry and with trade unions. His interventions were usually extremely brief and in a homespun style. He only once took a leading part by seconding an amendment, which he did with almost unmatchable brevity. His longest intervention, of one *Hansard* column length, was against the 1922 Jarrow Extension bill when he was clearly putting the view of the County Council. He was to reminisce that he had been asked at one time to stand as a Unionist candidate in Ireland yet his views appear to have been invariably critical of government policy during the post-1918 troubles in Ireland. The one most prominent subject of his questions in parliament concerned British military and police 'reprisals' and 'illegal methods'. Typical was the question he asked on 28 April 1921 about the numbers of women and of children under 16 killed and wounded by members of crown forces since the beginning of the year. Of 81 oral answers to questions he put, 25 concerned violence against what is now usually referred to as the nationalist population. Of 42 written answers to questions he put, twelve were on that subject. Of the 81 oral answers to his questions, only six directly related to constituency or County Durham affairs. There were more relating to the operation of the Safeguarding of Industries Act and German imports. Of the 42 written answers, only one concerned County Durham and the coal industry, but again there were several under the Safeguarding of Industries Act and the quantity and value of German and other imports. He retired from the seat in 1922, whereafter it fell to Labour, the Conservative candidate Anthony Eden coming second and the incumbent Liberals last. He lost his aldermanic office to Labour in 1925. He believed Socialism to be 'fatal' to working men's interests. Samuel Galbraith died on 10 April 1936.

Bibliography

Durham Chronicle, 16 September 1921; 20 January 1922; 21 March 1925; 24 October 1930; 17 April 1936.

Hansard's Parliamentary Debates, volumes 120–1, 125, 133–5, 138–48, 150–7.

Northern Echo, 30, 31 March; 5, 7, 8, 14, 16 April 1915.

Who Was Who, 1929–40, p. 487.

H. J. Smith

William Stephen Gilly (1789–1855)   Canon of Durham and Vicar of Norham

William Gilly was the son of the Vicar of Hawkedon in Suffolk. In 1799 he was sent to a boarding school where he was beaten and half starved. In 1802 he went to Christ's Hospital school where flogging was routine. He was ordained in 1813 and married in 1814. In 1817 he became the non resident rector of the tiny parish of North Fambridge in Essex. In the same year he published anonymously a book called *Academic Errors* protesting against brutalities in English Public schools. In 1822 his wife died leaving him with three small children.

Gilly's reaction was to set off on the Grand Tour. Presumably he left his children with his parents in Hawkedon. He decided to begin with a visit to the Vaudois valleys of Piedmont because he had learned about this ancient Italian Protestant community at a meeting of the S.P.C.K. in London. This trip changed Gilly's life and led to both the renaissance of the Vaudois church and to Gilly's appointment as a Canon of Durham Cathedral.

The Italian Vaudois (or Waldensians) are the most ancient surviving Protestant community in the world. They should not be confused with the inhabitants of the Swiss Canton of Vaud. In about 1200 AD they split from the Catholic church and formed their own Christian community. By the 1560s the Vaudois were following Calvinist practices. Thrice, in 1561, 1655 and 1686, they survived attempts at extermination organised by the Dukes of Savoy. Milton's angry sonnet 'On the Late Massacre in Piemont' is one of the bitterest poems in the English language. Throughout the 18th century the surviving Vaudois were restricted to three small alpine valleys.

Gilly was fascinated by the Vaudois. He spent six weeks in January and February 1823 recording the daily lives of these hardy peasants. In 1824 he published *Narrative of an Excursion to the Mountains of Piemont in the year 1823 and Researches among the Vaudois, or Waldenses, Protestant inhabitants of the Cottian Alps*. This book was a best seller and was reprinted several times.

For the rest of his life Gilly championed the Vaudois. For over thirty years he was Secretary of the London Vaudois Committee which he set up in 1824. The committee is still operating in 2000. He raised money in England for the construction of a Vaudois theological college in Torre Pellice (the only Vaudois town) and organised the rebuilding of Vaudois churches, an hospital and an orphanage.

Gilly was convinced that the Vaudois were the pipeline for continuous Apostolic Succession from Christ's Apostles to the 19th century without passing through the Catholic church. This claim is not now upheld by the Vaudois church as there is no record of the separate existence of their church before 1200 AD.

In 1824 Shute Barrington was Prince Bishop of Durham. Bishop Barrington was ninety years old and a redoubtable Anti-Catholic who kept alive the spirit of "No Popery". Whenever the chance arose he placed anti Catholic clergymen in the more lucrative livings in the diocese. Barrington was concerned that both Catholicism and radicalism were increasing in County Durham. Ushaw College had been established in 1800 for the training of Catholic priests and from his castle window Bishop Barrington looked down upon "Popish Elvet" which, even during the most stringent of the penal years, had retained a substantial Catholic presence.

Bishop Barrington read Gilly's book about the Vaudois and was impressed. Such an energetic priest would obviously be an asset to the Anglican cause. So Gilly, who had remarried on 18 December 1825, was nominated for a vacant cathedral stall. Bishop Barrington died at the age of 91 on 25 March 1826 and Gilly was installed as Prebend of the Ninth Stall of the Cathedral on 19 May 1826. He also was allocated a house (and free coals) at No. 9 The College.

In July 1826 Gilly was inducted as Perpetual Curate of St. Margaret's Church, Durham. It was normal practice for canons to hold such an additional living. St. Margaret's then attracted "vagrants and loose and suspicious characters who passed along the Great North Road". Gilly soon had 160 children in his Sunday school. He was so pleased with his success in catechising these children that in 1828 he published a book entitled *An exposition of the Duty and Advantages of Public Catechising in Church*.

William Van Mildert was installed (by proxy) as Prince Bishop of the Palatinate on 30 May 1826. He was an energetic Anglican traditionalist who saw it was his duty to defend the Church by Law Established. Gilly took his full share in the work of Durham Cathedral. He was Sub Dean on several occasions and proceeded to sort out the old charters and rolls which had been "in a great state of inter-mixture and confusion". In May 1827 he was present at the opening of the tomb of St. Cuthbert and indeed appropriated a piece of this precious relict.

Gilly also took an active part in the affairs of Durham City. In 1828 he set up the "City of Durham Society for the Suppression of Mendicity". He was president for eight years. This society was designed to "remove vagrants and impostors from the City by relieving the deserving and securing relief only to those who are really distressed". He was chairman of the Durham Auxiliary Bible Society in 1828, and on 29 October 1830 he proposed a motion at a meeting in Durham town hall urging Parliament to abolish slavery in the colonies as soon as possible. Years later a correspondent in the *Durham Chronicle* pointed out that Gilly wanted the slave owners to be compensated for loss of their property but did not advocate the payment of compensation to the negroes for having been made slaves. In 1828 he was President of the Durham Athenaeum and Chairman of the Durham City Interim Board of Health. He also took a significant part in the Ragged School movement and in the formation of Durham Penitentiary.

In 1835 Gilly published *Our Protestant Forefathers* when he returned to the subject dear to his heart of continuous Apostolic Succession through Vaudois. This caused a local controversy. For early in 1836 the Reverend James Wheeler (Priest at the Catholic chapel in Old Elvet) published *A Brief Reply to the Revd. Dr. Gilly's Tract*. This witty pamphlet complimented Gilly on his well known "mildness and suavity of disposition" but poked fun at Gilly's determination "To have none but Protestant forefathers". Wheeler went on to write "as to dismounting you from your Waldensian (Vaudois) hobby, believe me, my good Sir, I am not so ill-natured as to do any such thing, as it is a source to you of much pleasure, besides being a subject of no small amusement to many of your readers".

Gilly was involved in the controversies which accompanied the setting up of the University of Durham in 1832–33. The University was founded by the Bishop and the Chapter who funded the foundation professors, and gifted Durham Castle and other buildings around Palace Green. Gilly would have preferred the creation of an Anglican theological school as an initial step. Later however he came to accept the University as an integral part of Durham life and indeed arranged for three Vaudois students to study there.

In its early years Durham University was strongly Anglican. On 22 July 1833 Gilly wrote to Lord Brougham, the Lord Chancellor, that "The good ship The Durham University, was launched on Saturday last" and that the ship's company consisted of four professors, eight lecturers, two tutors, twenty students, and a bursar. Most of the academic staff were of course members of the Established church. However, with some reluctance, the Dean and Chapter appointed a dissenter to the post of Lecturer in Chemistry (J. F. W. Johnston). Gilly justified this departure from strict Anglican principles on the grounds of expediency.

Bishop Van Mildert, the last of the Prince Bishops, died on 21 February 1836. Gilly walked beside the coffin at the funeral procession in Durham Cathedral. On 19 March 1836 the Dean and Chapter met formally to elect his successor as Bishop. They had of course to elect the Government's nominee who was Dr Edward Maltby, Bishop of Chichester. However Gilly requested that the following protest should be entered into the minute book of the Dean and Chapter:–

"Considering that the act of electing a Bishop, as the Law now stands, is not a free act on the part of the Chapter, but one of compulsion, I protest against the use of any expression in the forms adopted upon this occasion, by which the Holy Name of God is invoked, which implies freedom of Election."

On 20 July 1831 the Dean and Chapter presented Gilly to the parish of Norham in North Durham. North Durham was then an isolated part of the county adjacent to the Scots border. At the same meeting it was resolved that "In future no one be presented to a living in the gift of the Dean and Chapter but on the understanding of residence, and that any person holding a Chapter Living presented to another in the gift of the Chapter do resign the first living forthwith". So he resigned as Perpetual Curate of St. Margaret's Church, Durham and at last, as Rector of North Fambridge which Essex parish had not seen him for years. However he remained as a very active Canon of Durham Cathedral.

He was an outstanding vicar. In Berwick-upon-Tweed Museum there is a life size effigy of him preaching an indignant sermon complete with a 'voice-over' in a strong local accent. He wrote theological books about his Apostolic Succession beliefs and of course was as active as ever in his work for the Vaudois. Working with his friend the architect Ignatius Bonomi he enlarged Norham church and constructed a Chapel at Duddo. He became a magistrate and lobbied hard (and unsuccessfully) against the incorporation of North Durham into Northumberland.

Gilly is still remembered as a champion of the agricultural labourers in Northumberland. For the local landlords appeared to be more concerned with the breeding of their cattle than with the living conditions of their hinds. In 1842 he abandoned prudence and wrote *The Peasantry of the Border – An Appeal on their Behalf*. This short, indignant, and powerful book is amongst the best of his many publications. He wrote:–

> "While some are directing attention to the flora, to the minerals, or to the romantic localities of this fine Border District, and others ... to the construction of cow byres, pig-styes, and sheep-folds, and to the irrational animals that are to occupy them, I will ... beg a few minutes' thought, in behalf of the cottager and the tenement which is prepared for him; and of the provision which ought to be made for the culture of his mind and for the advancement of his comforts, as a moral and immortal being."

A Hind's Cottage from
Gilly, William Stephen, *The Peasantry of the Border*
(Bratton Publishing Ltd., 1973, out of print)

He proceeded to point out that the practice of short term hiring of labourers meant that there was no stability in the lives of the hinds. Thus their children did not get proper schooling and their wives never knew where they would be living in a few months' time. This book was published first in Berwick-upon-Tweed in 1841 and was reprinted in London in 1842, and in Edinburgh in 1973. It is the only one of Gilly's books to have been reprinted in the 20th century.

In his sixties Gilly remained very active. In May 1855 he made his sixth journey to Piedmont to see the new Vaudois church in Turin. He was feted in the Protestant valleys. On his return he addressed two thousand people at the opening of extensions of Berwick-upon-Tweed Church on 26 August 1855. But a few days later he had a stroke and died on 10 September 1855 in his vicarage at Norham. When the news of his death reached Piedmont he was mourned by hundreds of Italian peasants as their benefactor and friend. In 2000 he is still remembered in the Vaudois valleys of Piedmont. Indeed several villages have a 'Via Gilly' – just as they have a 'Via Garibaldi'.

Bibliography

William Stephen Gilly, *The Peasantry of the Border*, 1973, Bratton Publishing Ltd., out of print. (Planned to reprint in 2001)

Prescot Stephens, *The Waldensian Story*, 1998, The Book Guild Ltd., Sussex, in print.

Hugh Norwood

| Frank William Goodyear (1873–1950) | Alderman and Mayor of Durham and Builder |

F rank William Goodyear was born at Orchard Street, Birtley, in the County of Durham, 19 March 1873, the son of Charles Goodyear, house plasterer. He was married at the Wesleyan Chapel, Chapel Passage, Old Elvet on 17 September 1898 to Isabella Scarr, daughter of John Scarr, coke drawer, of Dragon Villa, Belmont. They had two sons, Frederick Charles (born 30 January 1903) and Norman (born 7 May 1904).

His family moved to Dragon Villa, Belmont, where he was educated under Mr. Corbett. After leaving school he became an apprentice to John Shepherd, builder, of Gilesgate. At the age of 18 he was a brick factory labourer (1891 Census). Up until the age of 20 he attended building construction classes which were held in the University Lecture Hall on Palace Green. An advertisement in *Gilesgate Methodist Church, Centenary*

Celebrations 1869–1969 lists the firm as being established in 1894. His first houses were built c.1895 from plans and specification prepared by himself. He built extensions to St. Hild's, St. Bede's, St. John's and St. Chad's Colleges. In 1904 he is listed at 11 Malvern Terrace, Sherburn Road. He built this street and named it after the birth-place of his parents, Malvern, Worcestershire. On 11 May 1904, he gave an estimate to the Trustees of Elvet Wesleyan Church for the building of the caretaker's house, the cost being £295 (DRO M/DDV/1205). By 1916 he was living at The Gables, Gilesgate, a fine town house which he built overlooking The Racecourse. His eldest son was then attending Durham School, a clear indication of his prosperity. The Church of the Ascension at Easington Colliery was built by him in 1928 (consecrated 5 May 1929). The County War Memorial below the Rose Window at the east end of Durham Cathedral, was erected by this firm (1928). Two examples of his public building are the Palladium Theatre, Claypath, and The Fighting Cocks Hotel, South Street. The last location for the builders' yard was in Claypath, behind the former General Gordon public house. In *Kelly's Durham Directory 1938* the firm is described as: builders, joiners, undertakers, shopfitters, brickmakers and owners of the Tursdale Brick and Tile Works.

F. W. Goodyear's first step towards a long political career came on 26 February 1909 when he stood for the Gilesgate Ward against R. W. Salkeld, an old Gilesgate stalwart. Goodyear was victorious by 47 votes. He retained this seat for the Moderate Party, despite repeated contests, until 1930, when he was raised to the Aldermanic bench. When he was elected Mayor in 1916 he gave his workforce the day off with full pay. As Mayor he attended no fewer than 1,011 meetings. One of his highlights of 1916 was when he accompanied Field Marshal Viscount French as he inspected over three thousand men of the Durham County Volunteer Regiment in Durham Market Place. In 1916, a Mayor's Fund to honour the local heroes of the war who had gained military distinctions was started by him. It was later decided to present them with illuminated address from the citizens of Durham (see M. F. Richardson, *Durham: The People and The Place* (1994), 14). During the Great War, 1914–18, he was a special constable and group leader for the Gilesgate Ward. In the 1920s he instituted money-raising schemes (e.g. a pageant) for the preservation of Durham Castle. He was President of the Chamber of Trade, Chairman of the Governors Sherburn Hospital, and involved with the Gilligate Trust and Henry Smith's Charity. He was elected to Durham County Council in 1924. In 1926 he was Mayor for a second time. As a gesture of goodwill he organised a social event in the Town Hall for his workforce. He was appointed Justice of the Peace in 1928. *The*

Northern Echo, 8 May 1930, gives vigorous report on his protest against conference expenses by delegates from Durham County Council. He was a strong advocate of the building of new council houses, Goodyear Crescent on the Sherburn Road Estate was named after him for his service on the housing committee.

F. W. Goodyear, from a photograph supplied by M. F. Richardson

During his two terms of office he frequently spoke out in support of 'Durham for the Durhams' (i.e. 'transferring the headquarters of the Durham Light Infantry from the north to the south of the Tyne and near to their natural home by the Wear' (*The Durham County Advertiser*, 19 November

1926). The Regiment finally arrived at Brancepeth Castle during the Second World War, 1939-45.

His greatest honour was when he received the Freedom of the City on 4 October 1945 at the same time as The Right Honourable Anthony Eden. His illuminated scroll on vellum was specially designed; it shows a watercolour of Durham Castle, to commemorate the service performed by him in the restoration of that ancient building. This was presented in an oak casket made from the beams of Durham Cathedral and lined with white watered silk.

He was a prominent local preacher on the Wesleyan Circuit. His other interests included membership of the Norman Lodge of Freemasons (a former Master) and the Dunelm Lodge of Mark Master Masons.

His last public appearance was early in 1950 when he struggled to the window of his room in the Dunelm Hotel to view a civic procession to Elvet Methodist Church.

He died 6 April 1950, aged 77, at the Dunelm Hotel, Durham, where he had lived with his wife for several years. His funeral service was held in St. Nicholas's Church and conducted by the Revd. J. W. Wenham, assisted by the Dean of Durham, Dr. C. A. Alington, and the Archdeacon of Durham, the Ven. G. de Lucas. The Dean described him as 'a man of endless energy and unceasing vitality'. Representatives from all walks of Durham city life were present. Four of his employees were underbearers; he was taken to Newcastle for cremation.

Bibliography

Durham Record Office M/DDV/1205.

Gilesgate Methodist Church, Centenary Celebrations 1869–1969.

Goodyear Papers (Gilesgate Archives).

Kelly's Durham Directory 1938.

The Durham County Advertiser, 19 November 1926.

The Northern Echo, 8 May 1930.

M. F. Richardson, *Durham: The People and The Place*, p. 14, 1994.

Michael F. Richardson

Thomas Michael Greenhow M.D., F.R.C.S. (1792–1881) Surgeon

Thomas Michael Greenhow was born at North Shields on 5 July 1792. The son of a North Shields doctor, he grew up at his father's surgery and took his medical diploma at Edinburgh University. On 5 August 1814, he became a Member of the Royal College of Surgeons and, in 1817, was appointed surgeon at the Lying-in Hospital in Newcastle where he acquired considerable experience in obstetrics.

Nonetheless, surgery was his main interest, so he joined Dr. (later Sir) John Fife in establishing the Newcastle Hospital for Diseases of the Eye in 1822. Thereafter, his career was one of undeviating success.

When he first qualified, General Practitioners charged highly for dispensing their own medicines, and little or nothing for professional attendance. To redress the balance, Greenhow published a pamphlet, in 1824, arguing that doctors should charge a modest fee for attendance and a bare remuneration for medications. Next year, he wrote a more ambitious work recommending vaccination against smallpox and expressed his anger at the reactionary attitudes of his older colleagues.

In 1832 he was elected Surgeon and later Senior Surgeon at Newcastle Infirmary where he remained for some 23 years. Here, Greenhow's surgical success was noteworthy. Before antiseptic appliances were in general use, he recommended the importance of a pure atmosphere, of local cleanliness, and simple cold water dressings. These he preferred to the more usual ointments and lotions in the treatment of fractures and serious wounds. His success as a lithotomist was legendary, while his concern for the welfare of his patients and their post-operative treatment added considerably to their chances of recovery.

Possessed of considerable mechanical ingenuity, Greenhow developed or modified various instruments and surgical appliances. In 1833 he devised a fracture bed for supporting broken legs, which, for many years, was used at the Newcastle Infirmary at Forth Banks, and, until recently, at its successor, the Royal Victoria Infirmary. On 15 August 1848, he successfully performed one of the earliest operations of complete excision of the os calcis for caries of the bone. His surgical ability was recognised when he became one of the first surgeons to receive the Fellowship of the Royal College of Surgeons in 1843.

His pioneering views on sanitation and hygiene are equally noteworthy. During the cholera epidemic of 1832, he worked assiduously to alleviate the disease and published his views at considerable length. In 1852, he wrote to the Mayor of Newcastle, deploring the evils of overcrowding; of burying the dead in the midst of a populous town; of general uncleanliness; of imperfect drainage and impure air. He correctly prophesied a second visitation of cholera which took place the following year.

Education was another subject of his lasting interest. When a meeting was held in Newcastle, in 1825, to establish local infant schools, Greenhow became secretary of the resultant Newcastle Infants' School Society. Nonetheless, his main interest was medicine, so, predictably, the education of his own profession was his prime concern.

Following a national trend to promote a wider interest in literary and scientific subjects, the Literary and Philosophical Society was founded in Newcastle in 1793. This became the seed bed for the development of many of the region's learned institutions which, eventually, became the modern University of Newcastle upon Tyne.

In 1802, Thomas Bigge, one of the Literary and Philosophical Society's Vice Presidents, urged the establishment of institutions based on 'the application of scientific principles to the process of trade and manufacture'. Unfortunately, Bigge's proposals were too visionary during the war with France.

In April 1831, Greenhow continued the debate when, again at the Literary and Philosophical Society, he proposed the establishment of a College of Science in Newcastle. Had his plan succeeded, Newcastle would have followed London's lead in establishing an institution of higher education, free from religious tests, thus pre-empting the Anglican initiative for a University in Durham.

Greenhow endorsed Bigge's proposals in recommending instruction in the higher branches of mathematics, classical languages, literature and general science. His concern for his own profession was apparent when he included Medicine as well as Mining, Law and General Arts in his proposed curriculum.

Unfortunately, the plans for his designated 'University of Newcastle' were doomed to failure. More powerful battalions were being mobilised in Durham. On 31 August 1831, within weeks of Greenhow's proposal, the Dean of Durham warned of the adverse effects of the Reform Bill on the Church in Durham. Was this his sole concern, or did the Newcastle proposals expedite his plans? Certainly, when Bishop Van Mildert expressed disquiet at 'any mongrel affair at Newcastle', the Durham scheme proceeded with alacrity. The Royal assent was given on 4 July 1832, and the first students were admitted in Michaelmas term 1833, enabling Durham University to become established while Newcastle wrangled in committee. Nevertheless, Greenhow, supported by the local press, continued to argue that the Durham developments did not 'supersede (those) proposed for Newcastle, particularly the medical part'. The argument was valid, since Durham was based largely on Theology, whereas Greenhow contemplated Physical Science and Medicine in an institution redolent of University College, London, being non-resident and free from religious tests. As Bigge foresaw thirty years earlier, Newcastle did possess the nucleus of a university through its learned institutions, while local specialist knowledge was readily available for those destined for management in the mining, engineering and chemical industries. Unfortunately, no one provided the necessary funds.

Greenhow looked in vain for support from two eminent Northumbrians – Charles, Earl Grey, the Prime Minister, and John Scott, Lord Eldon, the Lord Chancellor. Nevertheless, even without their support, Newcastle's middle classes, for whom the college was intended, could have done more to help themselves.

In the event, the matter rested for forty years, until another generation, representing the interests of both Durham University and the Newcastle business and professional community, took up the cause. Dr. William Lake, Dean of Durham, and Warden of Durham University, supported by Durham University College of Medicine in Newcastle, convened series of meetings under the chairmanship of the Tyneside industrialist, Sir William (later Lord) Armstrong. These resulted in the opening of the College of Physical Science in Newcastle in October 1871. After being renamed the Durham University College of Science, then Armstrong College, it merged with the College of Medicine to form King's College, the Newcastle Division of Durham University. This, in turn, became an independent university in 1963.

Thus, Greenhow's visionary curriculum with its emphasis on Mining and Engineering, on Medicine, Law and the Arts, can now be seen as the blueprint for the modern University of Newcastle upon Tyne.

Meanwhile, in 1855, Greenhow was awarded the degree of Doctor of Medicine by Durham University in recognition of his outstanding services to surgery. Later the same year the Convocation of Durham appointed him to the newly established Chair of Medical Ethics, which he held until his retirement in 1860.

Greenhow stood at the interface between the old society and the new. He aligned himself with the progressives in their quest for popular education; for public health and welfare and for municipal reform. In his own field of surgery he not only saw the need for the highest standards of clinical practice but for education at university level. In this regard, he was a pioneer. Few of his contemporaries acknowledged that such standards of education were equally desirable in other areas like law, mining and engineering. Only financial constraints prevented these laudable objectives being achieved during his professional career.

Nonetheless, in October 1871, exactly a decade before his death, the first students were admitted to the College of Physical Science in Newcastle which, with the neighbouring College of Medicine, played such a distinguished part in the development of the Universities of Durham and Newcastle upon Tyne.

Thus the region's reputation for academic excellence in Medicine, the Applied Sciences and the Arts owes much to Greenhow's foresight and pioneering endeavours.

Truly, he was, 'A man born out of time'.

Bibliography

Anon., 'T. M. Greenhow', *Monthly Chronicle of North Country Lore and Legend*, Vol. V, June 1891.

Anon., Obituary Notice T. M. Greenhow, *British Medical Journal*, Vol. II, 12 November 1881.

G. R. Batho, 'A Man of Science: James Finlay Weir Johnston, 1796-1855', *History of Education Society Occasional Publication*, No. 5, 1980.

D. Embleton, *History of the Medical School, Newcastle upon Tyne from 1832-1872*, Newcastle, 1890.

D. Embleton, (Ed.), Papers Relating to Newcastle upon Tyne College of Medicine, Vols. I & II.

J. T. Fowler, *Durham University*, 1904.

R. M. Glover, *Remarks on the History of the Literary and Philosophical Society*, 1843.

T. M. Greenhow, *Lecture read to the Literary and Philosophical Society of Newcastle upon Tyne*, 5 April 1831.

T. M. Greenhow, *Lecture*, 'Additional Considerations', 7 June 1831.

G. Grey Turner, & W. D. Arnison, *The Newcastle upon Tyne School of Medicine 1834–1934*, Newcastle, 1934.

N. Hans, *New Trends in Education in the 18th Century*, 1966.

G. H. Hume, *The History of the Newcastle Infirmary*, Newcastle, 1906.

W. E. Hume, *The Infirmary, Newcastle upon Tyne 1751–1951*, Newcastle, 1951.

I. Inkster, and J. Morrell, (Eds.), *Metropolis and Province. Science in British Culture, 1780–1850*, 1981.

Literary and Philosophical Society of Newcastle upon Tyne, *Annual Report*, February 1832.

S. Middlebrook, *Newcastle upon Tyne. Its Growth and Achievement*, Newcastle, 1950.

D'Arcy Power, *Plarr's Lives of the Fellows of the Royal College of Surgeons of England*, 1930.

C. Preece, 'The Durham Engineer Students of 1838', *Proceedings of the Institution of Electrical Engineers*, History of Engineering Weekend Meeting, 6–8 July 1979.

Royal College of Physicians, *Annals*, Vol. 25, pp. 43–44.

Royal College of Surgeons, Minutes of Council, 16 June 1853.

R. S. Watson, *The History of the Literary and Philosophical Society of Newcastle upon Tyne, 1793–1896*, 1897.

R. Welford, *Men of Mark 'Twixt Tyne and Tweed*, Vol. II, 1895.

C. E., Whiting, *The University of Durham. 1832–1932*, 1932.

E. L. Woodward, *The Age of Reform, 1815–1870*, 1938, Second Edition 1961.

A. I. Short
T. W. J. Lennard

Cassy M. Harker (1912–1996)   SRN, Hospital Matron

The last ever Matron of Darlington Memorial Hospital and possibly the last Matron in the whole of the National Health Service, Cassy Harker began her nursing career at the age of 19 in 1932. She retired in 1974, the year of a major reorganisation in the NHS. During that period, revolutions in health care, hygiene, medicine and surgery had changed almost beyond recognition, and hospitals with them.

Her 40-year span of devoted service began at a time when leeches and maggots were still in common medical use, and nursing training had changed little since first laid down by Florence Nightingale in 1860. Nursing was still a vocation, a spinsterish sisterhood of middle class ladies living a cloistered life in the Nurses' Home. Their role was as the handmaidens of doctors. Consultants were regarded as demi-gods. Matrons were tyrants devoted to running hospitals with rods of iron. Nursing had nothing to do with money. Nurses received an 'allowance', and should be grateful for what they were given. Nursing was a duty and a calling, not paid employment. Until the Second World War to marry meant they had to resign.

Cassy Harker came of a strongly Methodist family and lived above their chemists' shop in Horsemarket, Barnard Castle. She started work at the shop on ledgers, and at 18 was apprenticed to her father, intending to qualify as a pharmaceutical chemist.

Describing herself as tom-boyish, obstreperous and strong-willed with an obstinate streak, she had been inspired at 16 by a book on the missionary nurse Mary Slessor of Calabar, and in 1932, at 19, she left to become a probationary nurse at Leeds General Infirmary, a teaching hospital where nurses were trained for three or four years, but not paid. They had to buy material and make their own uniforms. Three months in training school were followed by four years on the wards as student nurses working 7.00 a.m. until 9.00 p.m. and including menial work.

In 1938 she joined the Queen Alexandra Military Nursing Service. She was better paid and had better living standards, yet she could not stand the red tape and hierarchical divisions of status, and left during her probationary period to take a Theatre Sister's post in Mansfield General Hospital where treatment for mining accident injuries were a feature.

By 1940 Miss Harker was back at Leeds General Infirmary as Ward Sister on a female surgery ward, followed by work with children, male surgical patients and London bombing casualties. In 1942–43 came the bombing of Leeds by returning enemy aircraft, causing blast shock and collapsed lung injuries. From 1943 she was again a Theatre Sister, this time dealing with horrendous war injuries which brought a rapid development in surgical techniques. A need for nurses quickly led to the relaxing of old rules, and by 1943 nurses were able to 'live out'. That year's Rushcliffe Report changed nursing from a vocation to a profession open to all. In 1942, the Beveridge Report outlining the Welfare State boosted war-time morale. Cassy Harker became Theatre Superintendent in charge of all nursing teams, of the training of Theatre Nurses and of equipment. About 1945 she became an activist in agitation for better pay and conditions for nurses, backed by the Royal College of Nursing.

C. M. Harker, from a photograph supplied by Vera Chapman

After four years she transferred into nursing administration as Office Sister, and showed her flair as organiser and campaigner. The beginning of the National Health Service brought constant change through to the mid-1970s, including separate managers' offices for catering, laundry, nurse allocation etc.. She became in turn First Assistant Matron and Deputy Matron. In 1949, she moved to Chester City Hospital as Matron. This was a neglected ex-Poor Law Hospital. She helped to re-organise the Chester Royal and Chester City Hospitals under the NHS and "proved that a poor municipal hospital could be revamped and modernised".

In 1952 she was invited to move to Northallerton where the new Friarage Hospital was to be created out of an old workhouse and a collection of huts of a former Royal Air Force hospital. An administrative system, staffing and a training school were established, and a human and friendly hospital emerged with strong support from the town.

In 1962 Cassy Harker was appointed Matron to Darlington Memorial Hospital, where organisational changes were needed in order to catch up with the rapid advances in nursing, medicine and hospitals. A former voluntary hospital opened in 1923 as a memorial to victims of the First World War, by the 1960s it served patients from a large area stretching from Upper Teesdale to the edge of industrial Teesside and including south Durham and the then North Riding of Yorkshire. It managed a group of other local hospitals – Eastbourne, Hundens, Greenbank, Richmond and the Richardson Hospital at Barnard Castle.

But medical and senior nursing staff felt subordinate to administration. Cassy argued for a better voice for nurses in planning and decision-making as one of the three key sections of the Hospital Management Team. She championed the position of nurses in the Management system. She was Matron during the rapid expansion of Darlington Hospital, which included a new accident and emergency unit, nurses' residences, a 150-bed psychiatric unit, a 600-bed extension and the first coronary care unit in a North-East non-teaching hospital. In 1963 when she came, there were 300 nurses and 600 beds. When she retired in 1974 there were over 700 nurses and nearly 1000 beds.

Faced with the problem of loneliness, the only member of Senior Management expected to live on the job, she took a working break, applying for and winning in 1966 a Commonwealth Nursing Scholarship for three months in the USA and Canada to study nursing organisation and education in major cities.

There followed a period of exhaustion and depression from overwork and constant coping with change. Nurse became patient. She points out that she had spent the first half of her Darlington service fighting to get Matron recognised as a part of Senior Management and the second half presiding over her own replacement by an entirely new management system which came with the NHS massive reorganisation in 1974. Hospitals now meant health, not death. Preventive medicine meant fewer young patients with rickets, infections and deficiency diseases. Most patients were middle-aged or elderly, except for accident and emergency.

After 40 years' service of which 25 were in senior positions, her earnings were little more than a newly-qualified teacher at that date. She was asked to stay an extra two years until the 1974 NHS reorganisation. Fortunately the Halsbury Report recommended a salary increase from £2000 to £4000 per annum, which also meant a pension increase based on final salary.

Cassy Harker was recalled to help at the Friarage Hospital in Northallerton for the next three happy years, but by this time 'Matron' was a vanished title and a vanished species with a long and honoured tradition. 'Matron' means 'mother'. Cassy's organisational skills as well as her fighting spirit helped to achieve much for her nurses, as instanced by the *Northern Echo's* headline (13 December 1969): "Matron leaves her sick bed to stand by her nurses".

In an active retirement Cassy lived in Heighington. She is remembered as the enthusiastic Chairman of the Friends of Darlington Civic Theatre during its resurgence under the management of Peter Tod, which is where the writer shared with her some enjoyable social occasions.

Another happy retirement project was her book *Call Me Matron*, written in collaboration with her nephew Jack Glattbach, former deputy editor of the *Northern Echo*. She related with disarming frankness the vicissitudes of her life and work, of hospital politics, the struggle for overdue recognition of the nurse's role and the stresses involved in coping with constant change. She died peacefully in a nursing home in Barnard Castle close by the shop where her life began.

Bibliography

Vera Chapman, *Northallerton in Old Photographs*, Alan Sutton Ltd., 1994.

Darlington & Stockton Times, 27 January 1996.

Cassy Harker with Jack Glattbach, *Call Me Matron*, Heinemann, 1980.

Kenneth C. McKeown, *A Tale of Two Citadels*, the Pentland Press, 1994.

Northern Echo, 13 December 1969.

Vera Chapman

Thomas Heaviside (1828–1886)   Photographic artist

Thomas Heaviside was born in the parish of St. Oswald, Durham. He was the son of John Heaviside, schoolmaster, and his wife, Mary, and was baptised on 2 September 1828. The family lived in Court Lane, off New Elvet. Nothing is known of his education and early life. In 1851 he was living in Claypath with his widowed mother, three sisters and a brother, one of several families at number 14. His mother was a laundress, and Thomas' occupation was coach trimmer. There were two coach builders in Durham at the time, John Carnes and Hodgson & Co., both in New Elvet.

from the Heaviside collection in the archive at Beamish

On 13 March 1853, Thomas Heaviside married Ann Wilson at St. Nicholas church, Durham. In 1859 and 1860 he was still a coach trimmer, now living in Paradise Lane, off Claypath. In 1861 he and Ann had five children and still lived in Paradise Lane. His occupation was photographic artist. In 1863 he moved to Queen Street (now Owengate) and ran his business there until his death.

It was claimed that he was the first to set up a photographic business in Durham. He became well known for his views of the Cathedral and was one of the leading photographers in the north. He was also acclaimed for his *carte de visite* photographs which were popular at the time. In 1860 he photographed a presentation parade of the 7th Durham Volunteers on Palace Green. *The Durham County Advertiser* of 1 June reported: 'Mr Heaviside, the clever photographist of this city, took a photograph of the ceremony from the roof of the Cathedral ... with a view of having a woodcut from it inserted in *The Illustrated London News*.' The picture was published in *The Illustrated London News* of 23 June 1860 with the attribution 'our engraving is from a photograph by Mr Heaviside of Durham'.

Some of his work has survived including photographs of the Cathedral nave before the Gilbert Scott chancel screen was put in place. The screen was part of an extensive renovation of the Cathedral and the building was reopened with great ceremony in October 1876. Subsequently the sermons preached on the occasion were published. The review of this volume in *The Durham Chronicle* notes 'The frontispiece consists of an exceedingly fine and rich illustration of Durham Cathedral from the north from a photograph by Heaviside.'

He was a well known figure in Durham and, an obituary noted, 'his kindly disposition and good nature ... made him a very popular acquaintance and an always warm and trusty friend.' He was a member of the volunteer choir at the Cathedral but he took no active part in public affairs.

He and his wife had a family of eight children. Their eldest son John was a grocer. He married Ann Fawell and moved to Sacriston. Their son Michael served in the Royal Army Medical Corps in the Boer War. *The Durham County Advertiser* of 12 January 1900 published a letter from Michael to his father in which he described his experiences at the Battle of Magersfontein. On the outbreak of the Great War he joined the 15th Battalion, Durham Light Infantry and served as a stretcher bearer. He was awarded the Victoria Cross for bravery at Fontaine les Croisilles, France, on 6 May 1917. A street in Durham is named after him.

Thomas Heaviside's second son, Michael, was educated at Durham School and served his articles as a solicitor with H. J. Marshall, Market Place. He was taken into partnership by Mr Marshall and acted on behalf of the Miners Association in numerous cases. Although he had been disabled from infancy he was a leading member of Durham Amateur Rowing Club. His physical handicap made it impossible for him to row, but he often acted as cox. He was treasurer of Durham Amateur Rowing Club and acted as a short course judge at the Regatta. He died in 1885 at the age of 30. At his funeral at St. Mary-le-Bow church, rowing club members acted as carriers and six solicitors were pall bearers. The third son Thomas was educated at

Durham School. He died at the age of 19 in 1876. The fourth son Frederick worked for an architect. He briefly took over the photographic business when his father died, but he too died at the age of 29 in 1890. The fifth son James died at the age of 14 in 1877.

Thomas Heaviside died at his home in Queen Street on 27 January 1886. The funeral took place at St. Mary-le-Bow church and he was buried at Elvet Hill Cemetery. In his will he left £5,939 19s. 7d., a considerable sum in those days. After Frederick Heaviside's death in 1890 the business was taken over by A. F. Hayden, photographic artist. Close by at 53 Saddler Street was another photographer, W. McLeish. He was succeeded by E. J. H. Sercombe, and, in 1897, by J. R. Edis. When the Edis business closed in 1964 a large number of glass negatives remained in the shop. Some of these can be attributed to Heaviside. A few are marked 'Heaviside photo' and some can be dated to a period before J. R. Edis arrived in Durham. So although the two businesses did not occupy the same premises it appears that some of Heaviside's stock was transferred to Edis' shop. Photographs by Heaviside can be seen, and copies obtained, from the photographic archive at Beamish Museum and there are examples of his work at Durham University Library.

Bibliography

Census Returns, Durham City, 1851, 1861, 1871, 1881.

Durham Light Infantry Museum.

Durham Probate Records Register 1886.

Parish Register, St Nicholas, Durham 1853.

Parish Register, St Oswalds, Durham, 1828.

The Durham Chronicle, 12 January 1877; 17 July 1885.

The Durham County Advertiser, 1 June 1860; 29 January 1886; 12 January 1900.

The Illustrated London News, 23 June 1860.

Walker's Durham Directory 1848–1897.

Walker's Directory, Necrology 1887.

Audrey Kelly

Henry Heavisides (1791–1870)   Printer, poet and polemicist

Henry Heavisides, 'Printer, Radical and Poet' as the centennial edition of his collected works described him, was born in Darlington in 1791 and was educated at the Grammar School there. His mother ran a private boarding school in the town and his father, to whom Henry was apprenticed, a printing and bookselling business in High Row. Ill health forced Heavisides senior to retire just as Henry came out of his time but the poor state of the business offered no opportunity for him to stay in Darlington. He worked for the *Leeds Mercury* and in the important North Riding printing centre of Stokesley, before joining Christopher Jennett in Stockton-on-Tees. Here he remained as a journeyman printer and, subsequently, manager for forty-two years. Finally, at the age of 64 he set up his own printing business in Finkle Street.

Heavisides was a noted working-class intellectual who was involved in almost all progressive developments in Stockton during the mid-nineteenth century. He lectured widely, particularly through the Mechanics' Institute movement and took a prominent role in local radical politics, for example in the Queen Caroline agitation of 1820, the Reform Crisis in 1830–32, and the earliest phase of Chartism (from which he withdrew however because he disagreed with the use of 'physical force'), the Anti-corn Law League and Co-operation. 'But it was in the county elections,' his daughter recalled, 'that my father's energy and endurance were seen. He would set and print the election bills during the night, and lead the band during the day, besides writing election squibs and rallying voters.' When Stockton became a parliamentary borough in 1867, Heavisides was a formative influence on the emergence of the Liberal Party which secured the election of Joseph Dodds against Vane Tempest.

Heavisides was a prolific poet and a local historian of some note. A collection of poetry, *The Pleasures of Home* appeared in 1837, a historical survey of lyrical poetry from Shakespeare to Tennyson, *The Minstrelsy of Britain*, in 1860 and a curious collection of popular lectures entitled *Courtship and Matrimony* in 1864. *Annals of Stockton Tees*, the most enduring of his works, appeared the following year and is especially useful as a source of information about popular culture, institutions and politics in the town. Heavisides also taught basic literacy classes at the Stockton Mechanics' Institute, acted as the South Durham correspondent of the *York Herald* and engraved the illustrations for Brewster's *History of Stockton*.

Perhaps if he had concentrated on just one of his many interests Henry Heavisides might have met with wider fame. He was, though, the very epitome of the Victorian civic patriot and sought no reputation beyond Stockton. In the space of a short biographical essay it is difficult to portray the full significance of what he accomplished for Stockton-on-Tees since his sphere of influence was at the tier which tends not to be well-documented, below that of the town's councillors and magistrates and major employers. As a radical political activist his career stretched back to the Napoleonic Wars and, as his surviving political squibs reveal, he was a combative polemicist. His restraining hand upon local Chartism (reported in the *Gateshead Observer*, 27 July 1839 when he addressed a Market Place rally at some risk to his personal safety) was therefore all the more significant. It came at one of the few points in the Victorian period that class antagonism was widely apparent in Stockton, with troops billeted in the town and members of the local middle classes forming an armed volunteer force. However, for most of his life Heavisides appeared in the press, if at all, writing about others, or was reported in a couple of lines as lecturing or giving a recitation. Perhaps it was as a popular educator that he was most significant.

Henry Heavisides died in Stockton on 8 August 1870.

Bibliography

Malcolm Chase, 'Chartism, 1838–58: responses in two Teesside towns,' *Northern History*, 25, 1988.

Centennial Edition of the Works of Henry Heavisides of Stockton-on-Tees. With a Memoir Written by his Daughter, Mrs. Jane Heavisides Simpson, London, privately printed, 1895.

Malcolm Chase

Arthur Henderson (1863–1935)   Labour Party Leader

A rthur Henderson, three times the Labour Party's leader, its first ever Cabinet minister (1915–17) and, later, Foreign Secretary (1929–31), was very much a politician whose political roots were in the North East. He came to represent a solid, reliable, moderate Labourism which was comparable to Stanley Baldwin's very English Conservatism.

Yet, like David Lloyd George, 'the greatest Welshman ... since the age of the Tudors' (according to Churchill), Henderson was not born in the area associated with his name. Lloyd George was born in Manchester but brought up in Wales. Henderson was born in Glasgow but grew up in Newcastle (from the age of eight or nine). The facts about his origins are not fully clear. It seems he was probably born on 20 September 1863 to Agnes Henderson, a domestic servant. His mother married Robert Heath, a policeman, in Newcastle in May 1874. Arthur, his older brother and his younger sister grew up at Mill Lane and he attended school at Todd's Nook.

He was brought up in a Bible-reading household, with the family attending Congregationalist chapel on Sundays. At sixteen, after hearing the young Gipsy Smith speaking at a Salvation Army street meeting, Henderson became a 'born again Christian'. He found Christian fellowship at the Wesleyan Methodist Mission chapel on Elswick Road. In 1889 he and Eleanor Watson, one of his friends at the Mission, married. Together they had a long and happy marriage, bringing up four children, David, Will, Arthur and Nellie.

A. Henderson, copyright photo Elliot & Fry

Henderson was to be a major Nonconformist politician, beginning in the Liberal Party as a Lib-Lab but soon becoming a key figure in the early

Labour Party. While a young man, he taught in his chapel's Sunday school and took a very active part in its charitable and welfare activities. Later, he played a role in national Wesleyan bodies, especially the Wesleyan Methodist Union for Social Service and the Brotherhood Movement (of which he became President). He was also a much-travelled speaker for the North of England Temperance League before his election to Parliament.

Henderson was a big trade union figure in the Labour Party, though more party bureaucrat than his successor as the dominating front-rank trade unionist in the party, Ernest Bevin (in 1940–51). Henderson was from an 'aristocracy of labour' trade union – the Friendly Society of Iron Founders. He was apprenticed as an iron-moulder at the age of twelve, first at Clarke's Foundry and then, after it failed, at the Forth Banks Locomotive and General Foundry Works of Messrs Robert Stephenson and Son. After a one year interval in Southampton, Henderson worked for Stephenson's 1881–93. He was soon branch secretary of his union and in 1892 became its district delegate, responsible for Northumberland, Durham and Lancashire. He came to prominence within his union as the local official during a major iron-founders' dispute in March–September 1894. In these years in the North-East Henderson displayed his life-long preference for conciliation not conflict in industrial relations, and after the dispute he eagerly helped to set up a conciliation board for the iron industry. In 1902 he topped a national poll within the union for a Parliamentary candidate. From 1911 he was his union's President.

From his early adult years Henderson was active in politics. In Newcastle he was in harmony with widespread working class admiration for Gladstone, and was an admirer of the Liberals' 1891 'Newcastle Programme'. In 1892 he spoke as a working class supporter of John Morley at a big public meeting. That November he stood successfully as radical Liberal, backed by the Tyneside National Labour Association (which followed an 1886 TUC initiative to try to get more working men elected to Parliament), for the Westgate North council seat. In this by-election for Newcastle City Council Henderson proposed radical and trade-union measures, somewhat similar to those advocated by John Burns and the progressives on the London County Council. Henderson called for the council to be a model employer, paying trade union rates for work, observing the eight-hour day and avoiding sub-contracting 'which led to the pernicious evil of sweating'. He also called for the municipalization of the trams, gas and water. Once elected he was an eager supporter of a scheme to plant many trees on the Town Moor, thereby employing 200–250 men at a time of high unemployment (something he had experienced in 1884, 1885 and 1891).

In the 1890s in Newcastle Henderson was the epitome of the 'coming' working class Liberal. The national leadership of the Iron Founders was moderate, with Joseph Maddison, assistant general secretary then general secretary, having come from the North-East. Within the Liberal Party he had a powerful mentor in Robert Spence Watson. When in early 1895 John Morley wished for 'one in touch with the working classes' to run with him for the two member Newcastle Parliamentary constituency, Spence Watson secured Henderson's selection by 84 votes to 3 by the Liberal Party executive committee, but this was not ratified by the Liberal Thousand, who preferred the previous candidate, James Craig, a wealthy self-made man. Henderson accepted this verdict and, when the 1895 election was called, moved the resolution adopting Morley and Craig (who both lost).

Henderson's loyalty to the Liberal cause was rewarded by his being offered, and taking, the post of Liberal agent to Sir Joseph Pease, MP for Barnard Castle, from December 1895. In the previous two years he had worked for the *Newcastle Evening News*, set up in 1893 to 'fully recognise and advocate the wants of the workers'. Henderson and his family moved from 30 Croydon Road, Newcastle to 45 Hurworth Terrace, Darlington, moving later to Windsor Terrace. He took over a Liberal county council seat for a Darlington ward in March 1898 and that November won Darlington South ward to take a place on Darlington Council. In 1903 Henderson became Darlington's first Labour mayor, though council elections then were not fought explicitly on party political lines in the town.

Henderson's move to the Labour Party was due to the decisions of his union. The Friendly Society of Iron Founders was represented at the inaugural conference of the Labour Representation Committee (LRC) and its membership subsequently voted to affiliate by a two-to-one majority. Henderson was a delegate at the LRC's third annual conference in Newcastle. He became an early MP through chance: a by-election came up in his area, the Liberal candidate was unsound on the key issue of free trade; and the Conservative and Unionist government's popularity was sufficiently low to allow Henderson to win in spite of the split in the anti-Tory vote. His famous victory for Barnard Castle made him the fifth MP who acted in the House of Commons in an independent group of Labour MPs. However, until Labour's success in the 1906 general election (30 MPs) Henderson was ambiguous in his attitude to being independent from the Liberals. Thereafter, he was fully committed to the Labour Party and its independence.

However, from January 1906 he was primarily London-based. That month he moved his family from Darlington to Clapham Park. With substantial boundary changes at the end of the First World War he chose not to contest a County Durham or a safe Newcastle constituency but stood for East Ham South in 1918. This proved an unfortunate decision as he won and lost a succession of seats from then until his death in 1935: Widnes (1919–22), Newcastle East (1923), Burnley (1924–31) and Clay Cross (1933–death, 1935).

During his years as MP for Barnard Castle (1903–18) Henderson was chairman of the Parliamentary Labour Party (1908–10 and 1914–17), in effect party leader, and chief whip (1906–08 and 1914). He also began his long period as key party aparachtik, being party treasurer, 1904–11, and its secretary, 1912–34. He was the organiser of the restructured Labour Party of 1918, with a new and socialist constitution, revised policies and an improved party organisation throughout Britain.

With the outbreak of the First World War, Henderson, like most other leading trade unionists, supported the war effort. He helped recruiting and the organising of a massively increased munitions output, yet also promoted Labour's policies. He served as President of the Board of Education and then Paymaster General in Asquith's coalition government (1915–16) and was one of the War Cabinet of five under Lloyd George (1916–17), before resigning over his desire to support Kerensky's government in Russia by advocating that British Labour should participate in a proposed socialist conference in Stockholm (which, in the event, never took place).

After the First World War Henderson was very much the Labour Party's main organiser. In Ramsay MacDonald's first Labour government (1924), he served as Home Secretary. In the second (1929–31), with greater distinction, he was Foreign Secretary. With MacDonald's defection to the National government, Henderson became the Labour Party leader (1931–32), even though he, like nearly all its leadership, had lost his seat. From 1932–34 he struggled to secure world peace at the World Disarmament Conference in Geneva, as the world slipped towards war. In autumn 1934 he received the Nobel Peace Prize. He died a year later, on 20 October 1935, in London.

Bibliography

There were two early biographies by Labour MPs who knew him, E. A. Jenkins, *From Foundry to Foreign Office*, 1933, and Mary Agnes Hamilton, *Arthur Henderson*, 1938, of which Hamilton is better. There are two recent biographies, Chris Wrigley, *Arthur Henderson*, 1990, and the less archivally based, F. M. Leventhal, *Arthur Henderson*, 1989.

There are also valuable portraits in Mary Agnes Hamilton, *Remembering My Good Friends*, 1944; Margaret Cole, *Makers of the Labour Movement*, 1948; John Saville and Joyce Bellamy editors, *Dictionary of Labour Biography*, Vol. 1, 1972, and Morgan, K. O., *Labour People*, 1987.

Other important studies include David Marquand, *Ramsay MacDonald*, 1977; David Carlton, *MacDonald Versus Henderson*, 1970; Andrew Thorpe, 'Arthur Henderson and the British Political Crisis of 1931', *Historical Journal*, 31, 1, 1988, and Chris Wrigley, 'Arthur Henderson: From North East Industrial Conciliator to International Multilateral Disarmament', *North East Labour History Bulletin*, 25, pp. 5–24, 1991.

Chris Wrigley

William Hogarth (1786–1866)   Bishop of Hexham and Newcastle

William Hogarth, first Roman Catholic Bishop of Hexham and Newcastle, was born on 25 March 1786 of a small landowning family at Dodding Green, near Kendal, in Westmorland. With his brother Robert he was among the earliest students, in 1796, to enter the new northern seminary at Crook Hall, removed from Douai in France. His teachers included the historian John Lingard. He received the tonsure and four minor orders on 19 March 1807, the sub-diaconate on 2 April 1808, and after the College had removed to Ushaw in 1808, Bishop William Gibson of the Northern District ordained him deacon on 14 December 1808 and priest on 20 December 1809. As Professor and General Prefect, his students included the future Cardinal Wiseman. He was then Procurator or bursar, and his loyalty to Ushaw remained life-long.

In 1816 Bishop Gibson appointed Hogarth chaplain to the Witham family at Cliffe Hall, near Piercebridge, which included the care of Catholics in Darlington, and in 1824, Hogarth moved the mission to Darlington, where he built a church designed by Ignatius Bonomi and dedicated to St Augustine, adding schools in 1842, and a convent of the Sisters of Mercy in 1862. The Poor Clares moved to the town in 1857, another chapel SS Mary and Patrick, was opened in 1859, and the chapel of ease at nearby Gainford in 1852. The Darlington Catholic population grew from 200 in 1824 to 3,000 in 1866. In 1838, Bishop John Briggs of the Northern Vicariate appointed Hogarth a Grand Vicar or Vicar General, a position he held under Bishops Mostyn and Riddell in the new Northern District created in 1840. Riddell died in 1847 of typhus while administering to the immigrant Irish poor, and on 24 August 1848, at Ushaw, Briggs consecrated Hogarth Vicar Apostolic of the Northern District, with the title *in partibus infidelium* of Bishop of Samosata. In 1850, on the restoration of the English Catholic hierarchy of twelve bishops under a Cardinal Archbishop of Westminster, Hogarth became the first Bishop of the Diocese of Hexham, comprising the counties of Cumberland, Durham, Northumberland and Westmorland; the Diocese was renamed Hexham and Newcastle in 1861. As Bishop, Hogarth resisted the attempts by the new Bishops who had inherited parts of the old Northern Vicariate to parts of the inheritance of Ushaw College, a matter which involved him in years of litigation in Rome. He assisted the massive expansion of the College under the presidency of Charles Newsham, and offended his fellow northern bishops by his unilateral appointment of his old friend Robert Tate to succeed Newsham in 1863. His episcopate saw the expansion of the diocese from 70 priests, 51 public chapels and three convents in 1851 to 102 priests, 81 public chapels and 11 convents. There was a large growth in lay devotional organisations in the parishes. He was 'sensible and efficient, tireless too in the performance of his duties, all the while administering the Darlington mission', writes David Milburn. 'Rough and blunt, even uncouth in manner, if we are to believe the fastidious Lingard, he grew to some degree of greatness as an administrator of the District.' He had a horror of debt, and left his diocese largely free of it despite the poverty of its people.

Hogarth's long residence in Darlington, of more than forty years, his austere life and his unstinting charity to the distressed won him the respect of the townsfolk. Francis Newburn, the Anglican Borough Bailiff, describes Hogarth on his 77th birthday in *The Larchfield Diary* as 'my old and valued friend' of forty years: 'I do not know a more truly gentlemanly man, and a truer or better Christian does not exist.' Newburn also records that Hogarth had an unparalleled ability to disperse midnight revellers in public houses. A Darlington public house bears his name. He died in his 80th year on 29 January 1866. His congregation touched objects of devotion to his body in favour of cures, and the great Anglican parish church of St Cuthbert tolled its bell at his funeral. He was buried on 6 February in the then recently opened cloister of Ushaw College. A granite memorial in Darlington designed by Edward Pugin describes him as 'the father of his clergy and the poor, who by a saintly life, great labours and charity unbounded, won love and veneration from all.' He was affectionately known as 'Bishop Billy'.

Bibliography

Dictionary of National Biography.

Robin Gard, entry, *New Dictionary of National Biography*, still in ms.

Joseph Gillow, *A Literary and Biographical History, or Bibliographical Dictionary of the English Catholics: From the Breach with Rome in 1534 to the Present Time*, 5 vols., London, 1885–1902, vol. III, pp. 321–322.

Hogarth MSS, St Cuthbert's College, Ushaw.

David Milburn, *A History of Ushaw College*, Ushaw College, Durham, 1964.

Archives of the Roman Catholic Diocese of Hexham and Newcastle, (Letter Books, Status Animarum Records, Pastorals and other materials).

The Larchfield Diary of the late Mr. Newburn, First Railway Solicitor, Bailey, Darlington, and Simpkin, Marshall & Co., London, 1876, p. 186.

The Tablet, 10 February 1866.

The Weekly Register, 3 February 1866, 10 February 1866.

Sheridan Gilley

G. G. Hoskins, J P, FRIBA (1837-1911)   Architect

George Gordon Hoskins was an architect with a prolific output in the North East of England in high Victorian times. He set up his architectural practice in Darlington in 1864, and soon became one of only two Darlington-based practitioners at that period to be awarded a Fellowship of the Royal Institute of British Architects. He retired in 1907, having designed substantial buildings for public, private and commercial clients and for many of the region's wealthy entrepreneurs. These included the Quaker industrialists and bankers whose plain dwellings gave way to new mansions and parklands in town and countryside reflecting their status and prosperity. He also wrote three professional books.

Hoskins' designs included villas and mansions, schools and hospitals, chapels and cemeteries, assembly halls and hotels, shops and offices, banks and town halls, an exchange, a library, a museum, a technical college and a theatre. Working in a variety of styles and materials, his often flamboyant variants of Gothic, Queen Anne, Baroque, Renaissance and Baronial made a considerable impact on North East townscapes in contrast with the existing plain Georgian and vernacular buildings.

G. G. Hoskins, from James Jamieson, *Contemporary Biographies*, ed. W. T. Pike (Brighton: W. T. Pike, 1906)

He was born to a once-wealthy Staffordshire family which had been reduced in circumstances by the extravagance of his grandfather. George's father, Francis, became a captain in the Duke of Gordon's 1st Royal Regiment, and the duchess, realising the son's artistic talents, helped him to train as an architect. After practical experience with firms mainly in London and the South, George was appointed clerk of works to Alfred Waterhouse, the eminent Victorian architect and a Quaker, in the building of Pilmore Hall in Hurworth for Alfred Backhouse, 1863, and Jonathan Backhouse and Co.'s new bank premises on High Row, Darlington, 1864.

Hoskins' first and modest commission was the Temperance Hall in Hurworth, 1864. This was followed by designs for prominent families – Westbrook for Henry Pease, Elm Ridge and Woodburn for John Pease, Nestfield chapel for Robert Henry Allan, and Blackwell Hill for Eliza

Barclay. Other well-known buildings in Darlington include North Cemetery, the Grammar School, Crown Street Chambers, Edward Pease Free Library, Greenbank Hospital, King's Head Hotel, Technical College, North Star Offices and the Hippodrome and Palace of Varieties. His many others are less well-known.

Spread more widely across the North East, some of his notable buildings are or were Sunderland Gas Offices and the Victoria Hall, West Hartlepool Lynnfield Schools and Henry Smith School, banks in Sunderland, Bishop Auckland, Middlesbrough, Barnard Castle and Thirsk, and the Fleece Hotel, Richmond. His most widely recognised building, however, is Middlesbrough Town Hall and Municipal Offices opened in 1889 by HRH The Prince of Wales.

Some of his buildings have been demolished, giving way to urban redevelopment or changed social circumstances. Of those that can be attributed to him and survive, thirteen are today Listed Buildings. Research by the author is ongoing.

Bibliography

Vera Chapman, *Durham Archaeological Journal*, 4, 1988, 61–68 and 5, 1989, 65–69.

Vera Chapman, *Rural Darlington - Farm Mansion and Suburb*, Durham County Libraries, 1975, and High Force Publications, 1998.

Vera Chapman

Ralph Ward Jackson (1806–1880) M.P., founder of modern Hartlepool

Ralph Ward Jackson was the controversial mid-nineteenth century entrepreneur who, by initiating the building of both harbour facilities and a 'new' town on the west side of Hartlepool bay, could claim to be the chief founder of modern Hartlepool.

Like the far better known George Hudson, with whose career his own might be compared, he combined opportunism and entrepreneurial flair with a disregard for some of the niceties of financial legality; although in defence of both men it must be said that they operated in a period of intense business rivalry when the development of company law was lagging well behind the financial processes of industrial capitalism.

As the third son in the large family of a south Teesside landowner, Ward Jackson was sent to earn his living in the legal profession. In Preston, where he served his articles, he married the daughter of a Lancashire businessman and acquired contacts in the local business community. He returned to Teesside as a partner in a Stockton law firm, was appointed solicitor to the Clarence Railway company in which his father had been one of the early shareholders, and through this appointment became involved in the rivalry between the Stockton and Darlington and the Clarence railways and the complexities of the North East coal trade. (M.W. Kirby, *The Origins of Railway Enterprise: the Stockton and Darlington Railway 1821–1862.* (Cambridge, 1993) covers many aspects of that rivalry, albeit from the opposite viewpoint.)

His first apparent stroke of business initiative came when following the untimely death of Christopher Tennant (q.v.) in 1839, he 'took in hand' one of the non parliamentary lines being promoted to circumvent the opposition of the Stockton and Darlington company and the North East coal trade establishment to the extension of the Clarence network and the expansion of the coal shipping facilities at Hartlepool. (Direct quotations of Ward Jackson's perception of his own aspirations and achievements are taken from the speech he made on 2 October 1855 when he presented to the town the full length portrait of himself now hanging in Hartlepool Museum. The speech in its entirety is given in the appendix to Waggott pp. 207–9.)

The eight mile Stockton and Hartlepool link line was in itself a very minor undertaking but one of its corollaries was a proposal for a further coal dock at Hartlepool to the south of the existing limited installation. Rather than confront the inevitable opposition that a bill for a new dock project would provoke Ward Jackson managed to persuade the company already running the dock and harbour to take up its own parliamentary option to build an additional dock, at its own expense, to accommodate the anticipated flow of traffic along the new line. (The background to these manoeuvres may be found in W. Stokes' 'Regional Finance and the Definition of a Financial Region', E. Royle (ed.) *Issues of Regional Identity* (Manchester 1998) pp. 118–153.)

As railway development became the main motor of the economy in the early 1840s whether because of the insights provided by the various companies which he represented, or awareness of comparable instincts in his own personality, Ward Jackson seems to have been more alert than many of his contemporaries to the implications of the empire building activity of George Hudson. So it was that recognising the vulnerability of both the extensive but financially precarious Clarence railway system and the

Hartlepool Dock and Railway company on whose port facilities it depended, in 1843 he revived the scheme for an independent dock and in 1844 instigated the leasing of the Clarence to the Stockton and Hartlepool. (RAIL117/2 Special General Meeting of the Clarence Railway shareholders 20 August 1844; RAIL730/2 Hartlepool West Dock and Harbour Co. Minutes of Directors' meeting 1 July 1844.)

But as the Stockton and Hartlepool was, if anything, in a worse financial state than the Clarence, the next move had to be to find a well capitalised ally. Although there is no direct evidence that Ward Jackson was involved from the outset with the launch of the Leeds and Thirsk railway later the same year, that company's declared aims of linking Lancashire, the West Riding of Yorkshire and Teesside and the alacrity with which he responded to its approaches render it a possibility. (RAIL357/2 Leeds and Thirsk Board and Shareholders' Meetings 29 August and 17 October 1845.) Certainly he already had financial contacts in Leeds and through his father-in-law and his business associates, in Lancashire.

As negotiations with the Leeds and Thirsk advanced and the new independent Hartlepool West harbour and coal dock neared completion Ward Jackson began the promotion of a further dock scheme to provide accommodation for the anticipated more general merchandise that would use the linked railway system. (RAIL730/1 Hartlepool West Dock and Harbour Co. Annual General Meeting 30 September 1846.) But within days of the Hartlepool West Dock's opening on 1 June 1847 Hudson had blocked the parliamentary bill which would have legalised the amalgamation. (RAIL117/20 Clarence Railway letter book, letter of 12 June 1847.)

Although this was a cruel blow to Ward Jackson's immediate aspirations the move towards a more diversified traffic through the West dock system was more than vindicated by the effects of the repeal of the Corn Laws and of the Navigation acts. Despite continued opposition, the northward spur linking the West Riding of Yorkshire directly with Hartlepool was ultimately completed shortly after the opening of the merchandise dock in 1852, giving the textile towns what he had envisaged, an alternative shipping point to Hull.

In the meantime, however, it had required all Ward Jackson's business acumen to enable the linked companies within which he operated, to survive the repercussions of the nation-wide credit crisis of the autumn of 1847 which tumbled several overstretched northern joint stock banks and threatened a number of the collieries using the newly opened dock. Disaster was averted by providing 'temporary assistance' in the form of Stockton and Hartlepool company bonds and putting the leases of the collieries into the names of the resident viewers. Shortly afterwards by a similar sleight of hand Ward Jackson also acquired a threatened fleet of colliers and the supply contracts that went with them. (D/NRC/14 letter of 2 September 1848 Ward Jackson to Robinson Watson, a director of the Harbour company. RAIL730/48 Hartlepool W. Harbour and Dock Co. Accounts for collieries and ships starting October 1848.)

Hardly had the manoeuvre that eerily presaged that used against Ward Jackson himself some ten years later, toppled Hudson, although leaving his empire virtually intact, than it was discovered that a dissident group of Clarence shareholders was making advances to that company's long term rival, the Stockton and Darlington. Ward Jackson's response was to tighten the connection between the Clarence and the Stockton and Hartlepool by making the lease perpetual and to move toward a full amalgamation of the three companies in which he had an interest, once the second dock was completed. (RAIL117/18 Letters from Thomas Sturge, a Clarence director to his fellow Quaker and managing director of the Stockton and Darlington, Joseph Pease 10, 13 and 16 October 1849.)

Ward Jackson claimed in 1855 that his main interest had always been in the harbour installation, to use his own words 'Something to do with old Neptune and Boreas' and this is borne out by the way in which during the 1850s despite his other preoccupations, he pressed on with the construction of a timber dock and with an unrealised proposal for a harbour of refuge. His other preoccupations included supervising the creation of a 'new' town around the West harbour, which as early as 1851, was the subject of favourable comment for its 'spacious roads, neat and commodious shops and houses' and its 'effective system of sewerage and drainage'. (Procter p. 131.) By 1854 it also had an Improvement Commission chaired by Ward Jackson and a church built by subscription at his instigation. However the incumbent of the living and the Anglican authorities proved less amenable to his direction than the members of the Improvement Commission and an unedifying clash ensued. The details of this episode reveal not only his determination to be in control of what he increasingly saw as his creation, but also his intransigence in pursuing a resolvable issue to the bitter end, traits also evident in the events leading to his downfall.

There is a certain sad irony in the fact that while Ward Jackson was supervising the building of his 'new' town the Middlesbrough ironmasters Bolckow annd Vaughan were reinforcing the economic clout of his remaining local independent rival, the Stockton and Darlington company, by exploiting the same Cleveland ironstone seam that his own father had tried unsuccessfully to develop some forty years earlier. In the intervening period the demands of the railways and improved smelting and forging technology had changed perceptions of its value and the Middlesbrough to Redcar extension of the Stockton and Darlington line, intended primarily for recreational passenger use, was conveniently placed for the construction of a mineral branch to transport the ore to blast furnaces in Middlesbrough. (Kirby pp. 146–159.)

What followed was a competitive scramble to provide the means of exploiting the Cleveland ore field. Within months of the revelation of the new developments Ward Jackson had invited Bell Brothers, the Tyneside ironmasters, to occupy the now nearly redundant coal shipping site at Port Clarence and to take up the ironstone lease on the family estate at Normanby, but there remained the problem of transporting the ore from the mines to their blast furnaces on the north bank of the Tees, when the only mineral line into the area was controlled by the Stockton and Darlington and stopped short at Middlesbrough. So, by 1855, he found himself involved in trying to ensure independent access to the Normanby and other subsequently acquired ore measures by further railway initiatives and various schemes for negotiating the crossing of a river whose conservancy board was dominated by the rival company. (Tomlinson pp. 563–7.)

Despite the rancour generated by the measures and countermeasures employed by the rival companies over the transport of iron ore and the crossing of the Tees it seems unlikely that Ward Jackson's downfall was engineered by the Stockton and Darlington. It is much more probable that the initiative was related to the new round of takeovers and amalgamations that characterised the late 50s and early 60s. For at the time when questions began to be raised about financial irregularities in the operation of the West Hartlepool company the North Eastern Railway was negotiating a merger with the Stockton and Darlington, a move designed to pre-empt a similar approach from the rival North Western Railway; and as long as the West Hartlepool system remained independent there was every possibility of a counter merger between it and the North Western which would have presented an unacceptable challenge to the North Eastern's emergent monopoly in North East England.

It was Ward Jackson's own over-enthusiastic pursuit of a sordid financial matter involving his younger brother that opened the door to the questioning that undermined public confidence in the West Hartlepool company. This was accompanied by a vicious personal attack which forced Ward Jackson's resignation and a hostile blocking of the parliamentary measures by which the company sought to retrieve the situation. By 1865 the

Hartlepool network had followed the Stockton and Darlington into the hands of the North Eastern Railway.

Despite retaining local public confidence sufficiently to serve a term as the new constituency of West Hartlepool's first M.P. Ward Jackson's closing years were ones of loneliness and relatively poverty stricken decline. He died in London on 6 August 1880.

He remains a controversial figure, perhaps best considered as part of a generation of speculators and entrepreneurs who achieved much in the three decades that followed the opening of the Stockton and Darlington Railway in 1825 but whose style of operation was unsuited to the more regulated corporate capitalism of the second half of the nineteenth century.

Bibliography

The starting point for any examination of Ward Jackson's career remains :

Eric Waggott, *Jackson's Town – The Story of the Creation of West Hartlepool and the Success and Downfall of its Founder* (Hartlepool 1980) which along with an outline of Ward Jackson's life and business career gives the details of the 'Battle for Christ Church' and of the sequence of events leading to to his downfall.

In Durham Record Office the Newby Robson and Cadle Papers D/NRC contain some interesting examples of Ward Jackson's style of business.

John Procter's 1851 supplement to Cuthbert Sharp's 1816 *History of Hartlepool* (pbk Hartlepool 1998) gives a useful contemporary perception of the progress of the 'new town' and the West harbour to that date.

In the Public Record Office at Kew under the classification RAIL there are documents relating to all the railway companies mentioned and to the West Harbour and Dock Company.

W. W. Tomlinson, *The North Eastern Railway: Its Rise and Development* (first published 1915; reprinted Newton Abbot 1967) gives the history of the various lines that were taken over by the North Eastern including the Clarence, Stockton and Hartlepool and the Hartlepool Dock and Railway Company's line.

Robert Wood, *West Hartlepool* (Hartlepool 1967 pbk. 3rd edition 1996) covers many aspects of the town's history and devotes a chapter to Ward Jackson.

Winifred Stokes

James Finlay Weir Johnston (1796–1855)   Chemist and Educational Benefactor

Johnston, who was born at Paisley on 13 September 1796 and died at Durham on 18 September 1855, rose from modest circumstances to be acclaimed at his death as 'one who has done more than has ever yet been done to preach science to the masses'. (*Blackwood's Edinburgh Magazine*, November 1855, p. 548).

He undertook his University studies at Glasgow by self-help, particularly tutoring, and had a distinguished academic career there, winning prizes in Greek and Humanity, 1819–20; in Greek and Logic, 1820–21; in Mathematics and Ethics, 1921–22; and in Natural Philosophy, 1822–23 as well as Silver Medals for essays in 1824–25 and 1825–26.

He moved to Durham early in 1826 and established a private school in Claypath. In 1829 he married Susan Ridley who came from an old Northumbrian family and was some 19 years older than he. By now he was deeply concerned with chemical experimentation and he visited J. J. Berzelius, the great Swedish chemist, in 1829, moving on to Copenhagen where he met Ørsted, the discoverer of the magnetic effect of electric current, and W. C. Zeise, the discoverer of xanthates.

On his return to England, he helped to form the British Association for the Advancement of Science and was responsible for the record of its first meeting at York in 1831.

He was appointed Lecturer in Chemistry and Mineralogy at the newly founded University of Durham and became active within and without the University, earning a reputation as a man of outstanding ability. From 1844 to 1849 he was lecturer and chemist to the Agricultural Chemistry Association of Scotland and from 1848 to 1852 he taught Agricultural Chemistry to the students of the Diocesan Training College for Men at Durham. Perhaps however his most radical contribution was the part he played in establishing the first University course in Engineering in 1838 but few students enrolled.

Over the years Johnston consolidated his reputation as an experimental chemist. F.R.S. in 1837, his early work on plumbocalcite provided the first case of isodimorphism and he gave an important paper 'On Dimorphous Bodies' to the B.A. in 1837. He investigated the iodides and double iodides of gold, prepared mercuric cyanide in crystals, published extensive research on resins, obtained a sugar from eucalyptus manna which Berthelot later called melitose, and made a pioneering attempt to isolate cocaine.

J. F. W. Johnston, by courtesy of the *Johnstonian*

Johnston's principal claim to fame was as a prolific and popular writer. His *Catechism of Agricultural Chemistry and Geology* went through 37 editions in his lifetime. In 1849 he published an influential book on the use of chemicals in farming – *Experimental agriculture*. He went to North America 1849/50 and published *Notes on North America – Agricultural, Economical and Social*, 1851. His last work was his best essay in popularisation, *The Chemistry of Common Life* (2 volumes, 1856); despite its 800 pages the book was an immediate success and new editions appeared in both 1859 and 1879. The introduction demonstrates his educational stance:

What most concerns the things that daily occupy our attention and cares,are in early life almost sedulously kept from our knowledge.

He spent the summer of 1855 on the Continent, returned to Durham with a lung infection and died from its effects. In his last illness he desired to be buried in a country churchyard and chose Croxdale.

Johnston is remembered locally primarily not as a chemist but as an educational benefactor. He left the residue of his estate, after the death of his wife, to trustees 'to appropriate the same to such literary, scientific or educational objects as they ... deem most expedient'. Under that provision, the Johnston Laboratory was created in the Durham College of Science in Newcastle but little more had been done when the Reverend Thomas Randell, Principal of Bede College, and Mr. Alexander Scott, Physical Science Master at Durham School, complained to the Charity Commissioners in 1890. An investigation ordered the trustees to dispose of surplus money which had accrued and over £3,000 became available for the establishment of a co-educational technical school on a site provided by the trustees in South Street. The school has since evolved into a comprehensive school, now situated more salubriously on the west of the City.

Both as a chemist and as a benefactor Johnston deserves to be better remembered.

Bibliography

G. R. Batho, 'A man of science: James Finlay Weir Johnston (1796–1855)', published in *Biography and education: some eighteenth and nineteenth century studies*, History of Education Society Occasional Publications, 5, 1980.

Charity Commissioners' Report 1904, vol. 1.

Durham County Advertiser, 28 September 1855.

D. M. Knight, *Atoms and Elements*, London, 1967.

The Transcendental Part of Chemistry, Folkestone, 1978.

H. C. Knoblauch, et al., *State Agricultural Experiment Stations*, U.S. Dept. of Agriculture, 1962.

C. Preece, 'The Durham Engineer Students of 1838,' published in *Transactions of the Architectural and Archaeological Society of Durham and Northumberland*, new series 6, pp. 71–74, 1982.

R. Spence Watson, *The History of the Literary and Philosophical Society of Newcastle-upon-Tyne (1793–1896)*, London, 1897.

G. R Batho

John Kane (1819–76)   Trade Unionist

John Kane was born in Alnwick, Northumberland. Orphaned at an early age he was aged seven when he went to work, first in a tobacco factory and then as a gardener. At seventeen he moved to Gateshead to work at the mills of the iron manufacturers Hawks, Crawshay & Sons. A natural orator and resilient negotiator, Kane quickly became involved in workplace politics, founding a short-lived union for north Durham ironworkers as early as 1842. He was active in the later stages of the Chartist movement on Tyneside and went on to become involved in a range of radical initiatives, for example the Northern Reform Union, the Newcastle Working Men's Reading and News Room, the Gateshead Ratepayers' Association and the Cramlington Co-operative Society. Simultaneously, he worked his way up through the hierarchy of labour at Hawks, Crawshay & Sons to become a roller.

In the 1860s Kane became a household name across the North-East as leader of the National Association of Ironworkers (NAI), the trade union he founded in Gateshead in 1862. The cyclical fortunes of the iron industry, divisions between the many grades of workers and strength of the masters made this a difficult trade to organise. But the economic boom of the early 1860s (during which the iron industry especially benefited from the American Civil War) provided more propitious circumstances. The NAI achieved noticeable increases in wages for all grades of workers in a concerted two-week strike across the North East in 1865. On the other hand its appeal in the West Midlands, where there was a rival union, was slight and in West Yorkshire the NAI was defeated in a bruising six-month lockout in Leeds. For his role in this Kane was dismissed by his employers. Henceforward his only source of income was from the NAI and he carefully cultivated its North East stronghold. He did briefly move in 1867 to Staffordshire, taking the union's headquarters with him, in an unsuccessful attempt to extend its influence southwards but soon returned to County Durham, this time to Darlington where he remained for the rest of his life.

The context of this 1867 move was the momentous defeat of the NAI in the five month 'great strike' in the Cleveland and South Durham iron trade.

86

It reduced the NAI essentially to a union for the most skilled levels of the trade. The less-skilled blastfurnacemen withdrew their support and settled with the ironmasters after the first month of the dispute. Kane's standing in the NAI was undiminished, however, and in the years that followed he went on to play a key role in the development of an arbitration committee for the Cleveland and South Durham iron trade, in partnership with the Durham ironmaster David Dale.

In 1868 the NAI was retitled the National Amalgamated Malleable Ironworkers Association. The headquarters remained in Darlington but the union achieved a genuinely national coverage through a federal structure which incorporated the strongly regionalist trade union movements in the iron industry. Kane now became a major figure in British labour politics. He attended the inaugural conference of the TUC in 1868 and was an early chairman of its parliamentary committee. He gave extensive evidence, much of it concerning the Cleveland and South Durham iron trade, to the Royal Commission on Trade Unions. He was also a notable figure in Darlingon's civic life. He was a leading member of its Ratepayers' Association and Mechanics' Institute and was elected to the School Board.

Kane grew increasingly uneasy about the ability of organised labour to advance its circumstances, with workers still not directly represented in Parliament despite the 1867 reforms. Accordingly he welcomed the formation in 1869 of the Labour Representation League, whose aim was to support trade unionists as parliamentary candidates in key electoral constituencies. Kane's natural talent and extensive experience eminently suited him for Parliament and in September 1873 he was adopted as the League's candidate for Middlesbrough. Nationally, the League was wrong-footed by Gladstone calling a snap General Election the following January and only two of its thirteen candidates were elected. No attempt had been made to form constituency organisations and Kane was dependent upon his union and the Middlesbrough Temperance Society (he was a lifelong teetotaller) for his campaign. It was never going to be easy opposing Henry Bolckow, the Liberal ironmaster who had been returned unopposed in the borough's first parliamentary election in 1868 and who stood again in 1874. The situation was complicated by an Irish dimension that was never far from the surface in Teesside politics. During the Fenian scares of the late 1860s a considerable antagonism had developed between Teesside's Irish community and its neighbours, not least English and Welsh ironworkers. Kane's radicalism did not appeal to the local Roman Catholic clergy: opposed to Fenianism and anxious to do nothing that might jeopardise their Church's fortunes in a still-suspicious Protestant country, they directed voters to support Bolckow. The Irish vote was doubtless also influenced by memories of the 'great strike' just eight years before, the vast majority of Teesside's Irish ironworkers being blastfurnacemen.

Kane had the satisfaction of beating the Conservative, another ironmaster, for second place. Bolckow, however, was comfortably returned, helped by the support of the vast majority of electors who were Irish and/or blastfurnacemen. To compound Kane's disappointment the federal structure of the Ironworkers' Association itself began to unravel. By 1877 its activities were largely confined to Cleveland and Durham. Kane strove to keep the union together but the strain proved too much for his health. He died suddenly on 21 March 1876 and was buried in West Cemetery, Darlington.

Bibliography

Malcolm Chase, 'The Teesside Irish in the nineteenth century', *Cleveland History*, 69, 1995.

Nick Howard, 'Strikes and lockouts in the iron industry and the formation of the ironworkers' union, 1862–69', *International Review of Social History*, 18, 1973.

J. H. Porter, 'David Dale and conciliation in the northern manufactured iron trade, 1869–1914', *Northern History*, 5, 1970.

Eric Taylor, 'John Kane', in J. Bellamy and J. Saville editors, *Dictionary of Labour Biography*, vol. 3, 1976.

Malcolm Chase

Peter Lee (1864–1935)   Miner and trade unionist

Peter Lee worked in fifteen pits by the time he was twenty-one. Born in Trimdon in July 1864 into a family of eight children, he had only such snippets of formal education as constant movement from one school to another allowed. Beginning as a driver lad at Littletown working 10-hour shifts, he had tackled most pit jobs in most of the collieries of East Durham within the next few years. As he constantly had to prove himself to a new set of peers, he became 'one of the boys' – drinking, blaspheming and indulging in fist fighting. At 21, he was well over 6 feet in height, 'body steeled by hard labour, straight looking grey eyes set in a fine face, thick black hair curled around his cap' – but unfulfilled.

It was at Wingate, sitting in the Lanky House pub, that Peter Lee became convinced of the futility of his life so far, and he resolved to change himself so that he could help others. His plan for reform was simple – to stop drinking, swearing and fighting, and to get himself an education while looking for opportunities for service. He learned to read and write at evening classes and broadened his horizons by travelling abroad – his *grand tour* was of the pits of Pennsylvania, Ohio, Kentucky and South Africa.

On his return to Wingate, Peter Lee was denied a colliery house when elected checkweighman and served several more collieries in that capacity to become a good prospective candidate for a county union position. He was elected a member of the Durham Miners' Council and ultimately became Agent, then General Secretary of Durham Mineworkers. He acquired a national, and international, platform as he crowned Presidency of the National Federation of British Miners with Chairmanship of the International Miners Conference.

Peter Lee, from William A. Moyes, *Mostly Mining*
(Newcastle upon Tyne: Frank Graham, 1969) plate 26, opp. p. 123

When others wanted to settle wage agreements locally he wanted national agreement. "I don't want to think in districts. I want to think nationally. We have sought a national agreement and, for the time being, we have failed. Don't get it on to your mind that failure will exist forever ... let us plod on. Let the chaos caused by the coalowners, mismanagement, and indifference of the government deepen, as it will deepen, then public opinion will say that the endurance of the miners has been great under great difficulties." (R. Page Arnot, *The Miners in Crisis and War*, London, 1961, p. 125.)

He correctly assessed the mood of the miners when he condemned Ramsay MacDonald for his desertion of the miners. To his international audience in Lille he declared,

"In my own nation, we have a Prime Minister who once stood up for justice and right – a man of the people. He now associates with those who wear fine raiment, live in castles and have always been the enemies of the people." (R. Page Arnot, *The Miners in Crisis and War*, London, 1961, p. 197.)

MacDonald lost his Seaham seat to Shinwell in the next election.

Peter Lee recognised, at an early stage, that politics and trades unionism must go hand in hand in an area like Durham. There were those who thought differently (e.g. one lodge opposed Agents accepting political office) but they were defeated in a democratic vote. With a background of achievement in local government Peter Lee had no doubts at all and he used his powers to improve the appalling living conditions of working families. He became chairman of his parish council in 1903 and Chairman of the East District Council by 1909. His main local concerns were housing and sanitation and their effect on health. Election to represent Thornley on the County Council was followed by a unique situation when, in 1919, Labour had the majority for the first time and was faced with filling all the political offices with men who were inexperienced and untried. None had even been committee chairmen before. Who better than Peter Lee, who in local and union activities had done so much to win the respect of his fellow men, to elect as Chairman? So, at the age of 55, he was civic leader of County Durham, as well as union leader of the largest union. After a brief period in opposition, Labour was re-elected with Peter Lee as a very active leader until 1932. Opportunities to improve the lot of the families of working men now presented themselves. Of many achievements, none gave Peter Lee greater pleasure than the improvement to the water supplies represented by the construction of Burnhope reservoir and its distribution network, though good houses were equally important. "I have no hesitation in saying it is one of the worst districts in Britain as far as housing is concerned." (W. R. Garside, *The Durham Miners 1919–1969*, London, 1971, p. 287.) He also had a firm grasp of wider politics. At international conferences, he raged against fascism. "Comrades, stand up resolutely against Nazi rule: fight it with vigour. Everywhere the slogan must resound 'Down with Fascism – long live the organised working class." (R. Page Arnot, *The Miners in Crisis and* War, London, 1961, p. 196.) He was equally opposed to communism, especially in what he regarded as attempts to interfere with union elections.

Peter Lee stuck to his resolution for personal reform. The restrictive observations of the Methodism faith attracted him, and he embraced them fervently, becoming a local preacher in the ranter tradition. He was a natural leader and made good use of the rostrum. He died on 16 July 1935, and , although he had lived in Durham City for many years, he was buried (at his own request) in the village cemetery in Wheatley Hill which his political agitation had obtained three decades previously.

The memory of Peter Lee was still green in 1947 when the New Town in East Durham was named after him. The town of Peterlee was appropriately designed to solve many of those problems of deficient living conditions that had concerned the man throughout his life. Some forty years later, a bust of Peter Lee was unveiled in Shotton Hall, a fine (and perhaps final) testimony to a man of stature and influence.

Bibliography

R. Page Arnot, *The Miners in Crisis and War*, London, 1961, pp. 125, 196, 197.

W. R. Garside, *The Durham Miners 1919–1969*, London, 1971, p. 287.

Jack Lawson, *Peter Lee*, London, 1936.

W. A. Moyes, *Mostly Mining,* Newcastle upon Tyne, 1969.

W. A. Moyes, *Wingate, Community Centre*, Wingate, 1962.

W. A. Moyes

James Maw (1807–1875)   Chartist and temperance worker

J ames Maw was among the best-known of early Middlesborians and an
    influential figure in the South Durham Chartist movement. He was the
illegitimate son of the daughter of an East Cleveland brewer and grazier.
Some time before 1835 he migrated to Middlesbrough to work as a
bricklayers' labourer. A Methodist, he was apparently one of the founder
members of the Middlesbrough Temperance Society in 1834. An advocate
of total abstinence, he took a strong stance against others in the Society
(mainly Anglicans) who approved of moderate alcohol consumption, and the
following year led a splinter group of teetotallers into what was described as
'a pitched battle' in the Market Place against supporters of the drink trade.
The following year the Society switched to a policy of total abstinence and
Maw took a place on its committee which he occupied virtually
uninterrupted until his death.

   In Middlesbrough's earliest years, the control exercised by the Owners
of the Middlesbrough Estate over civic affairs was total. Before 1841 the
Temperance Society was the focal point for almost all popular political
activity since it was the only organisation permitted to hold open-air
meetings in the town. Maw steered the Society towards a close involvement
in Chartism, the national mass movement for parliamentary reform which
dominated so much of British politics in the late 1830s and 1840s. By this
means national political issues were discussed in the town, which made Maw
its delegate to the Council of the Durham Charter Association. Under
Temperance auspices Maw brought Chartist lecturers to address torch-light
meetings in the Market Place; he also played a leading role in setting up a
'Working Men's Reading Room', the first non-sectarian adult education
initiative on Teesside.

   Maw was also a prodigiously energetic Chartist propagandist in South
Durham and Cleveland: during the winter of 1839–40 he sometimes
lectured three or four times a day in different communities. He can be
variously glimpsed making 'a long argumentative speech' in Hartlepool
(quoting the legal theorist Blackstone and the economist Adam Smith),
leading the formation of a Teesside Chartist Council and trouncing the Anti-
Corn Law League in a set-piece debate. Yet he still found time for 'soap-
box' oratory in Middlesbrough Market Place each Saturday and he was still
a brickies' labourer.

   Although he continued to support Chartism his involvement in the later
phase of its history was more circumspect. He may have related less easily
to the more prosperous Chartists who contested – successfully on several

occasions – seats on the Middlesbrough Improvement Commission and subsequently the Corporation. By 1851 he had also changed jobs, employed by the Owners as agent in charge at the Middlesbrough coal staithes. Like so much of the working-class movement itself, Maw's political activism took on a more settled, perhaps even a class-conciliatory aspect. He was a founder member of the Middlesbrough Equitable Provident Benefit Building Society and in 1860 took a prominent part in the Teesside and South Durham labour movement's campaign against Tommy Tickets. This method of paying wages via tokens redeemable only at selected grocers contravened the Truck Act, but it took a concerted series of legal actions against the ironmasters before it was abandoned in the region. Maw condemned it as 'direct and downright roguery' and described Middlesbrough's civic father Henry Bolckow as 'one of the basest of hypocrites' for paying Tommy Tickets.

These comments are a fair specimen of Maw's combative rhetorical style. It is unclear whether it was this or his employment by the Middlesbrough owners that kept him off political platforms in the mid-Victorian years. But he could be relied upon to make a stirring speech from the floor, noticeably so in 1866 when he successfully hijacked a public meeting called by the Mayor (to advance the case for the town becoming a parliamentary borough) to move a memorial to the Queen and Prime Minister calling for the dissolution of parliament and a general election on the issue of universal suffrage. Active in the local branch of the radical National Reform League, Maw made his last recorded public speech attacking the proposed Reform Bill for its failure to embrace universal male suffrage and the secret ballot. Along with his bluntness and implacable opposition to anything that smacked of a patronising or dismissive attitude to working people, Maw seems to have been widely recognised as highly principled and scrupulously honest. Evidence for this can be seen in his election to the committee of the Middlesbrough Liberal Association, which thus gave him a hand in the election of Bolckow as the borough's first MP.

Maw died at his home on 18 September 1875 after a brief illness. His funeral was accompanied by a lengthy cortege in which the massed members of all three of Middlesbrough's temperance societies walked in procession. All the local papers carried substantial obituaries and there was widespread recognition that Maw had helped to define the political life of Teesside.

Bibliography

Malcolm Chase, ' "An influence to the rising borough of the Tees": James Maw, 1807–1875', *Cleveland History*, 71, 1996.

Malcolm Chase, 'Chartism, 1838–58: responses in two Teesside towns', *Northern History*, 25, 1988.

Malcolm Chase, 'Chartism and the "prehistory" of Middlesbrough politics', *Bulletin of the Cleveland & Teesside Local History Society*, 55, 1988.

Middlesbrough Temperance Society, *Souvenir: Centenary Celebrations, 1836–1936*, 1936.

Malcolm Chase

William Andrews Nesfield (1794–1881)   Soldier, Painter, Landscape Gardener

William Andrews Nesfield was born in Lumley Park, the eldest son of the Rev. William Nesfield, Perpetual Curate of St. Mary and St. Cuthbert, Chester-le-Street, and Elizabeth (née Andrews) of Shotley Hall, Northumberland. In 1808, after Elizabeth's death, the family moved to Brancepeth where William's father had been inducted Rector of St. Brandon's Church. In 1809, his father married Marianne Mills of Willington Hall whose nephew was to become the renowned Gothic revivalist architect Anthony Salvin. Subsequently the Nesfield and Salvin families were more closely linked through the marriage of William Nesfield's younger sister Anne to Anthony Salvin.

Nesfield was educated at Durham School then on Palace Green and Winchester College before he entered the Royal Military Academy at Woolwich as a Gentleman Cadet. In 1812 he was gazetted 2nd Lieutenant in the 95th regiment and served under the Duke of Wellington in the Peninsular War seeing action at San Sebastian and Waterloo. He exchanged into the 89th and was appointed ADC to Sir Gordon Drummond and joined him in Canada in 1814, having been shipwrecked on the Island of Anticosti *en route* for Halifax, Nova Scotia. He was stationed in Canada for two years and was at the defence of Chippewa. At the age of 21 years he retired from the Army on half pay and took up a career as a water colour painter. He had sketched and painted in Canada, including Niagara Falls and a back drop scene for a play on canvas 20ft x 14ft showing the Falls of Chaudiere. In

94

1819 and 1820 he toured France, Germany and Switzerland sketching, drawing and painting in the company of his patron Newbey Lowson of Witton Tower, Witton-le-Wear; Lowson had been J. M. W. Turner's patron and accompanied him on his first visit to the continent in 1802.

Nesfield was elected to the Old Water Colour Society and was taught by one of the members, Anthony Copley-Fielding. Between 1823 and 1851 he exhibited 91 paintings. Only a few paintings are in public collections and on display, but the Vicoria and Albert Museum holds a remarkable portfolio of 130 drawings, mainly pencil and watercolour of miniature size but exquisitely executed. A further 400 paintings are held by the family and many more were dispersed when Nesfield's office in York Terrace, Regent's Park was closed. The subjects of his watercolours are wide, ranging from buildings and animals to mountainous landscapes, seascapes and waterfalls. His paintings were noticed by John Ruskin, who wrote in *Modern Painters*, that in his execution of the Falls of Schaffhausen, (Nesfield) '... is a man of extraordinary feeling, both for the colour and spirituality of a great waterfall: exquisitely delicate in the management of the changeful veil of spray or mist; just in his curves or contours; and unequalled in their way.'

Whilst still exhibiting at the Old Water Colour Society, encouraged by his brother-in-law, Anthony Salvin, with whom he shared a house in London, he began work as a professional landscape architect. From 1840 until his death he was responsible either singly or with his sons, Arthur Markham and William Eden, for no less than 259 commissions in England, Wales, Scotland and Ireland. These included the Royal Botanic Gardens, Kew, Stoke Edith in Herefordshire, Crewe Hall in Cheshire, the Royal Horticultural Society's Garden in Kensington, Witley Court in Worcestershire, Castle Howard in Yorkshire, the Avenue Gardens in Regent's Park, Holkham in Norfolk and St. James and Green Parks. Nesfield re-introduced the formal elements of the seventeenth century to his garden designs – parterres, friezes, fountain basins, flights of stone steps, stone balustrades and pavilions: garden ornaments, especially vases and tazzas, designed by Nesfield were characteristic features. But there were many practical and novel features such as parterres on sloping ground so that they could be viewed not only from a terrace but also during a perambulation, and the use of pebbles around roses and shrubs as both ornament and to conserve soil moisture. His training in hydraulic engineering at Woolwich enabled him to design the water features that were so effective in many of his gardens. One of his greatest achievements was the design and laying out for Lord Ward of ten acres of garden ground at Witley Court to which he referred as his 'monster work'. He designed two parterres and two fountain bases – the Flora Fountain and the Poseidon Fountain – of which the latter was reputed to be the largest in Europe. It was carved from a single block of Portland stone by James Forsyth to a design by Nesfield. It comprised Perseus on the winged horse Pegasus rescuing Andromeda from a sea monster. The main jet of water issued from the mouth of the monster and rose some 120 feet. Subsidiary jets issued from the mouths of eight surrounding dolphins and reeds fitted into their mouths yielded a range of sounds.

Nesfield described himself as an artistical landscape gardener and contemporaries described him as the 'master spirit of the day'. He was the most sought after and effective Victorian landscape gardener laying out ground for private clients and for the public: he was probably the greatest of all the Victorian landscape gardeners whose work in Regent's Park and at Witley Court is now being restored.

Bibliography

A. Bury, 'A note on William Andrews Nesfield 1793–1881', *The Old Water Colour Society's Club 27th Annual Volume*, 1949.

B. Elliot, 'Master of the Geometrical Art', *The Garden*, 106, 1981.

Shirley Evans, 'Genius of the Pattern', *Country Life*, 12 May 1994.

Shirley Evans, 'Master Designer', *The Antique Collector*, October 1992.

Shirley Evans, 'Talented Twice Over', *Country Life*, 8 April 1993.

Shirley Evans, 'The Gardens of Witley Court' in Richard Gray, Jeremy Musson and Shirley Evans, *Witley Court, Hereford and Worcester*, English Heritage, 1997.

M. J. Tooley, 'William Andrews Nesfield 1794–1881,' Exhibition Guide, Witton-le-Wear, Co. Durham, Michaelmas Books, 1994.

M. J. Tooley, editor, 'William Andrews Nesfield, 1794–1881. Essays to mark the bicentenary of his birth,' Witton-le-Wear, Co. Durham, Michaelmas Books, 1994.

Michael Tooley

Charles Mark Palmer (1822–1907)   Merchant

Charles Mark Palmer was born on 3 November 1822 at King Street, South Shields. He was born into a prosperous family – his father, Mr. George Palmer, being a well-known merchant and shipowner on the Tyne. Fourth child in a family of eight children, Charles was educated at Dr. J. C. Bruce's 'Percy Street Academy' in Newcastle, completing his business education in the South of France, before entering his father's firm of 'Palmer, Beckwith and Co.'.

This grounding in his father's business no doubt prepared Palmer for his venture into the coke business. In 1845, at the age of 23, Palmer joined the firm of John Bowes, a wealthy coalowner. Shortly thereafter, Palmer went into partnership with John Bowes in the Marley Hill Coking Company and by the late 1850s the firm 'John Bowes and Partners' had expanded further, having acquired some 14 collieries. Thus, 'John Bowes and Partners' developed into one of the largest colliery concerns in the North of England, producing over a million tons of coal annually compared to 50,000 tons only a decade before. From the outset, Palmer displayed a natural penchant to make commercial ventures work. On the death of John Bowes, Palmer became Chairman and Managing Director of the Company. He retired from these positions in 1895, succeeded as Managing Director by his second son, Alfred.

Palmer also moved into the shipbuilding business. In 1851, Charles, aged 28, and his brother, George, took over a wooden vessel shipyard at Jarrow as 'Palmer Bros. & Co'. Palmer solved the problem of high transport costs of coalowners in the Great Northern Coalfields in reaching their London market, by developing the steam, iron screw-propelled collier, capable of carrying heavy loads at moderate speed and low costs. In 1852, Palmer built the steam powered, iron screw-propelled collier 'The John Bowes' and set up the General Iron Screw Co., of which he was Managing Director. So successful were his colliers that he became prolific in his building of these ships, it becoming the standing joke with his workmen that he 'built colliers by the mile and cut them off in the required lengths'.

In 1856, Palmer went from strength to strength when the Government commissioned for the Crimean War, the iron clad warship 'The Terror'. To meet the tight deadline of just 3 months, Palmer instituted one of the first uses of rolled iron plates, a much quicker process compared to the traditional forging method. This was the first of many warships built for the Admiralty and many foreign navies. He also built many cargo vessels, oil tankers and passenger vessels. The rapid extension of shipbuilding must have caused major problems, not least the provision of a steady supply of materials. In answer to this problem, Palmer ventured into many other enterprises making for total integration of the Company. For example, he leased the ironstone workings at Hinderwell on the North York Moors near Staithes and erected a harbour named Port Mulgrave where his ships could load. He erected, in all, 5 blast furnaces at Jarrow and by 1859 added forges and rolling mills. Many of his ships were engined by Palmer's engine works and he repaired them in the firm's large repair dock completed in 1865. In 1862, his brother, George, retired from the business and Charles sold his Company to the public and set up his limited liability concern of 'Palmers Iron and Shipbuilding Co. Ltd.', being Chairman and Managing Director. With his integrated concerns, the Company had grown in stature and scope. It was little wonder that Palmer was considered the founder of Jarrow, transforming the district from a small collection of dwellings in 1852 into a busy, prosperous town, its growth a direct result of his enterprise. Indeed, by the time of Palmer's withdrawal from the Company in 1893, at the age of 71, it had launched a total of nearly one million tons of shipping and the town had grown massively in population to about 40,000. The works by then covered some 100 acres with a river frontage of three quarters of a mile and a labour force of 7,500.

From the late 1860s, Palmer's involvement with the Company lessened as he spent more time on other matters, particularly politics. In 1868, he became liberal M.P. for South Shields and took a large share in the Tyne Plate Glass Co. at South Shields, later becoming sole owner of these glassworks. However, this new company proved a considerable drain on his resources and so this venture had to be wound up. In 1870, Palmer had a hospital built in Jarrow and although he handed over his duties soon after, he remained alderman until his death. In 1886, he was created baronet and was made Commander of the Order of St. Maurice and St. Lazarus of Italy in 1892. By 1904, a bronze statue was initiated by his employees and erected to him as a lasting tribute for all he had done in the town.

Palmer was a great entrepreneur of his time. He tried out new ideas, wanted to expand his empire and reduce dependencies by integrating ventures. Though he owned an estate at Grinkle Park in N. Riding, Yorks with nearly 4,000 acres of land, as well as houses in London and Newcastle, his association with Jarrow was immense as this was where he had made his fortune. Married three times, with five sons and one daughter, Charles Palmer died on 4 June 1907 at his London home.

Bibliography

Jarrow Express and Tyneside Advertiser, p. 7, 7 June 1907.

Sylvia Davis Furnues, 'Continuities and Contrasts in Education in Jarrow, 1944–1988', Ph.D., Sunderland University, 1998.

Sylvia Davis, 'Education, Industry and the Community: Jarrow Secondary School, 1911–1944', M.Ed., Durham University, 1991.

Sylvia Davis, 'The Evolution of a Jarrow Senior School, 1944 to 1974', M.A. thesis, Durham University, 1987.

Norman McCord, *North East England. An Economic and Social History. The Region's Development 1760–1960*, London, Batsford Academic, 1979.

H. Poulson, *Jarrow's Tribute to Her Founder. A New Song*, Newcastle upon Tyne, 30 January 1904.

J. B. Priestley, *English Journey*, Middlesex, Penguin, 1987 reprint.

D. J. Rowe, 'Palmer, Sir Charles Mark', *Dictionary of Business Biography*, vol. 4, Mc-R, *A Biographical Dictionary of Business Leaders Active in Britain in the Period 1860–1980*, edited by D. J. Jeremy, London, Butterworths, 1985.

Ellen Wilkinson, *The Town that was Murdered*, London, Left Book Club edition, Victor Gollancz Ltd., 1939.

Sylvia Davis Furnues

James Pigott Pritchett, FRIBA, (1830–1911) Architect

J. P. Pritchett junior was a well-known Victorian architect practising mainly in the North of England, particularly in County Durham and the North Riding of Yorkshire. He was best known for his churches. His Gothic designs were especially in demand for Church of England and Congregationalist communities. A tall, slender spire forming an urban or rural landmark in the region is likely to be of his design. One of his best known churches is St. Nicholas in Durham City's Market Place.

Pritchett was the son of James Pigott Pritchett senior (1789–1868), a prominent York Congregationalist and architect who succeeded to the practice of the famous John Carr of York and practised from there for 55 years. Pritchett junior was trained by his father and became a partner in 1853. In the following year he took over his brother-in-law John Middleton's practice in Darlington. He ran an active general practice from an office on High Row from 1854 until about 1910, although in failing health for the last five years. His son Herbert Dewes Pritchett who joined him about 1880 became a partner in 1900 and continued the business after his father's death in 1911.

J. P. Pritchett, from James Jamieson, *Contemporary Biographies*, ed. W. T. Pike (Brighton: W. T. Pike, 1906)

Because sons served in turn in their father's practice, it is not always clear who was responsible for particular designs. The dates of births and deaths of the two James, however, should allow the correction of simple mistakes in some printed accounts!

According to his obituary in *The Builder*, the work of James Pigott Pritchett of Darlington comprised 'seventeen cemeteries, chapels etc. in various parts of the country, 25 new churches, 20 restorations and additions to churches, 28 Non-Conformist chapels, 16 parsonages, 18 schools and Sunday schools, banks, a Training College at Darlington, offices, hotels and shops, and over 40 houses and cottages, and he was surveyor to the Cleveland Estate in Darlington.'

The Northern Echo obituary differs slightly in claiming '26 new churches, 4 banks, 12 offices, hotels and shops, restorations to 2 castles, and monuments and parish halls.'

Contemporary Biographies mentions 'upwards of 100 churches and chapels, 21 cemeteries, including Darlington West Cemetery, many schools and mansions and the restoration of St. Cuthbert's church chancel, Darlington and Raby Castle chapel.'

MARKET PLACE, DURHAM.

Durham 1857-8, by J. Pritchett, postcard of 1904 supplied by Vera Chapman

The Darlington and Stockton Times obituary does identify a few Darlington buildings, including St. Paul's church, the Congregational church, the Training College, the Savings Bank, St. Cuthbert's chancel renewal and houses on the Duke of Cleveland's Estate.

Certain of Pritchett's churches have received particular praise. For example, St. Nicholas, Durham, with the only Anglican spire in the city, was described at the time as 'the most beautiful modern specimen of church architecture in the north of England'. Pevsner/Williamson deemed it 'one of the best churches Pritchett designed', while Pocock and Gazzard thought it 'a place-marker of great architectural distinction' and 'the most impressive of Victorian churches in the city'. Pevsner regarded Christ Church, East Lyton near the A66, as 'a very serious piece of architecture', whilst Hatcher thought it 'the most impressive Victorian church in Richmondshire, of quality fittings and ashlar throughout thanks to a generous benefactor'. St. George's Presbyterian church in Sunderland in red sandstone was notable for a 'very original' lofty tower with the upper part 'all open under a pyramid roof supported by long uprights'.

Pritchett's characteristic spires could reach considerable heights, as at Scarborough Congregational 175 feet, Durham St. Nicholas 160 feet, Stockton St. James 130 feet and Whitby West Cliff Congregationalist 120 feet. Also with impressive spires in Sunderland were Grange (West Park) Congregational and St. Luke, Pallion (spire now removed). Tall, and especially outstanding on their hill-top sites, are All Saints, New Shildon, and All Saints, Great Stainton.

Impressive, too, is the size of some of Pritchett's churches, and not necessarily in the rapidly growing industrial towns. Sunderland's St. George's Presbyterian was for 1,200 but Scarborough's Eastborough Congregational was for 1,300 and its South Cliff Congregational for 1,040. Even in the small new resorts at Whitby West Cliff and Saltburn-by-the-Sea, Pritchett could design West Cliff Congregational for 950 and Emmanuel, by gradual accretion, served 1,000.

Smaller, mainly perhaps village churches, also came under his remit as at Denton for 100 and Reeth Congregational for 400, Darlington St. Luke's for 450, Cornforth Holy Trinity for 320 and St. Laurence at Middleton-St-George for 300. At Cockerton came St. Mary's by Pritchett and Son in 1900 with fashionable terra cotta dressings. Cemetery chapels were also small, and often won by competitions. Pritchett designed those at Ely, Darlington (West), Scarborough, Whitby, Bishop Auckland, Mansfield and Tottenham.

Of his secular buildings, Gunnergate Hall, Marton, near Middlesbrough, 1858, was for John Vaughan, partner of ironmaster Henry Bolckow and prover with John Marley of Darlington of the Cleveland Main Seam of ironstone. Together with his son Thomas's additions, the Hall was a

Victorian Gothic extravaganza, now no more. Also early was Pritchett's elaborate polychrome brick and scallop-slated villa, the parsonage behind John Middleton's 'railwaymen's church', St. John the Evangelist, at Bank Top, Darlington. The Savings Bank in Tubwell Row was Italianate, unusual for Pritchett. Pease and Partners offices in Northgate may have been his, or Ross and Lamb's. Certainly the Quaker families were behind his Darlington Training College for lady teachers, 1875, now the Arts Centre, and his later Arthur Pease School. In 1900 the old premises of Thomas Pease, Son and Company, tea and grocery merchants and latterly wine and spirit merchants in Darlington Market Place, were rebuilt to Pritchett and Son's red brick and yellow terracotta design. It was the bequest of the firm's Edward Thomas Pease that enabled Cockerton church to be built in the same year.

As agent to the Duke of Cleveland and then to the Lord Barnard for their Darlington Estate, Pritchett was responsible for the layout of a large area between Woodland Road and Coniscliffe Road west of Skinnergate, and therein designed at least 100 houses, some with his son. In restorations at Raby Castle chapel, Pritchett rediscovered ancient features, including the six-light screen which opened into the contemporary Barons' Hall. In the 1860s he had restored St. Cuthbert's chancel in Darlington, removed the flat roof and parapets, raised it to its original pitch and inserted seven lancet windows into his rebuilt east end. He also rediscovered the Saxon cross shaft at Croft-on-Tees. His expertise and interest in medieval architecture and archaeology was reflected in frequent lectures and writing.

Demolitions and casualties include Jarrow Congregational church, Sheldon Street; Stockton St. James, Portrack Lane; Sunderland St. Luke; Marton Gunnergate Hall; and in Darlington St. Luke, Leadenhall Street, St. John's Parsonage, the Wesleyan chapel (Northlands), North Road, and St. Paul's, North Road (burnt down). Of his more than half a century of output, however, a great number of Pritchett's buildings remain to enhance our landscapes and townscapes.

Bibliography

Vera Chapman, 'Thomas Pease, Son and Co: A Family Business and its Premises in Darlington Market Place,' *D.C.L.H.S. Bulletin* 31.

Darlington Borough Planning Applications.

Jane Hatcher, *Richmondshire Architecture*, C. J. Hatcher, 1990.

Lynne F. Pearson, *Building the North Riding: a Guide to its Architecture and History*, Smith Settle Ltd., 1994.

Nikolaus Pevsner, *The Buildings of England: County Durham* (1953); *Yorkshire: The North Riding* (1966); *Yorkshire: York and the East Riding* (1972); Nikolaus Pevsner and Elizabeth Williamson, *County Durham*, revised 1983, Penguin Books.

D. Pocock and R. Gazzard, *Portrait of a Cathedral* City, City of Durham Trust and Department of Geography in the University of Durham, 1983.

The Builder, Vol. 101, 29 September 1911.

Vera Chapman

A. E. Prowse (1880–1955)   Ministry representative at Elisabethville and surveyor

A Belgian settlement was created at Elisabethville, Birtley, both to house refugees and to find workers for munitions when a critical shortage occurred in 1915 and there is no doubt that this was a major contribution to the war effort. At one stage there was a population of 7,000.

Albert Edward Prowse, who became the administrator at Elisabethville in 1918 but was retained there from 1916, played a vital role in creating a happy working environment there and at another, smaller factory at Scotswood, Newcastle upon Tyne. He was made M.B.E. for his service and the King of the Belgians gave him the Order of Leopold, the equivalent of a knighthood. His family, after being housed at first in a bungalow on site, lived at Lambton House, adjacent to the Durham Road, until 1930; in the early years the children were taught by Belgian teachers and spoke French with a Belgian accent.

Prowse was the son of A. E. Prowse, senior, of Birchfield and educated at the Higher Grade School, Aston. He joined Chesshire, Gibson and partners, Estate Agents and Auctioneers, and became their surveyor 1900–1909; he was employed as a Sectional Valuer by the Valuation Office, Inland Revenue, Birmingham district, 1910–1915 and became a Ministry of Munitions Inspector in December 1915.

Albert Prowse was transferred from Birtley to the Office of Works in 1921, eventually becoming District Estate Surveyor at Manchester and retiring in 1948. He had been a Fellow of the Royal Institution of Chartered Surveyors from 1918.

One of his sons, Dr. W. A(rthur) Prowse (1907–1981) became first Master of Van Mildert College, Public Orator and Reader in Physics in the University of Durham as well as Lt. Colonel in the Officer Training Corps and a Deputy Lieutenant for the County.

Bibliography

Daily Chronicle, 21 February 1916.

Number Ten, Quarterly Magazine of Ministry of Works, N.W. Region, December 1948.

J. Schlesinger and D. McMurtrie, *The Birtley Belgians,* University of Durham History of Education Project, 1997.

University of Durham Gazette, Epiphany Term 1982.

Private papers by courtesy of Miss Clare Prowse.

D. M. Prowse, M.B.E., Childhood Memoirs of Elisabethville, an unpublished TS.

G. R. Batho

Thomas Ramsey (1812–1873)   Miners' Union Pioneer

D urham Miners, for their first really Big Meeting of 1872, chose Saturday, 15th June. To mark the occasion cannons boomed at the expense of one particular miner, 60-year-old Tommy Ramsey of Trimdon Grange.

How many times they roared and how much powder was expended remains obscure, but it cannot have been cheap for an old fellow who earned 28 shillings a week as an Assistant Agent and had to pay the expenses of running his district out of that. It must have been worth it – a jubilant exploded version of the noisy crake Tommy used to summon miners to meetings. Ramsey probably got the idea from the previous year's picnic of Durham Miners' Mutual Confident Association where he had been one of the speakers. It was held on 12th August, 1871 at Wharton Park high above Durham city where cannons were lodged on the ramparts. That day there was only a crowd of a few thousand to hear the speeches. Tommy's task, then, was to propose a resolution full of big words ('ameliorative agencies'!), obviously assembled by a committee with a dictionary on the table and reported verbatim by the newspaper. The gist was that the Union pledged itself to continue.

In the ten months since that first meeting, membership of the new Union had boomed and a larger space found to house the expected hordes of people, bands and banners. The Union was not yet three years old: the hated bond had been abolished four months earlier, coal prices were high and the miners thronging into the city had food in their bellies and money in their pockets.

It was a joyous time. Hope was in the air and it had not come too soon for Tommy Ramsey who had worked to get miners to combine for their own protection all his working life. His role had been as a rallying mascot, walking from village to village sounding his crake and persuading men to meetings. Many times he was beaten by bullies, but Tommy only got himself a new crake and went on with his task. Frequently he slept in the open because men feared they would be put out of their houses if they gave him refuge. After he spoke at a meeting in Thornley he was locked out of the pit but by then the union could come to the rescue and give him an official job.

Many of the pitmen in Durham that day knew Tommy Ramsey by sight, all by repute. He was as distinctive as Charlie Chaplin. He often wore a dusty black, big top hat and a very old fashioned suit with a long jacket with tails. Add a great white beard, worthy of an Old Testament prophet, and you have the right picture.

The main speakers in 1872 were William Crawford, agent of the infant association, Thomas Burt of the Northumberland Union, and Alexander MacDonald, president of the National Miners' Union. They were upwardly mobile men of the time who had learned to understand legislation, to speak with politicians, bargain with coal owners, and administer large funds.

Tommy Ramsey's strength was his single-minded belief that combination was strength. He got in a few words towards the end, moving a vote of thanks to the surgeon, Dr. Jepson, who had lent the miners the field next to the racecourse. The newspapers did not report his exact words this time, but it seems unlikely that on this one occasion he gave his recruiting speech. John Wilson, historian of the Durham Miners' Union, said Ramsey had one speech, and it invariably went something like this:

> 'Lads, unite and better your condition. When eggs are scarce, eggs are dear; when men are scarce, men are dear.'

Simplicity, says Wilson, was Ramsey's greatest eloquence. 'His words were few, but forcible: not polished, but very pointed – and they went home.'

For Tommy Ramsey it was nearly the end of the line. His closing words that day were recalled when the newspapers reported his funeral less than a year later. 'Lord, now let Thy servant depart in peace, for mine eyes have seen Thy salvation.'

He was reputed to have been a life-long advocate of a miners' union and associated with Thomas Hepburn of the short-lived union of 1831–32 as well as Martin Jude in the forties. Unlike Hepburn and Jude who are well documented but died in obscurity, Ramsey, who had never taken a central stage, was given a hero's send off. He had fallen on ice at his brother's home in Blaydon and died on 8 May, 1873 of bronchitis. His funeral was attended by miners' leaders and a contingent of fifty miners from Trimdon Grange whom he had represented in all the meetings leading up to the founding of the union. His statue, complete with crake, still stands in Blaydon Churchyard erected by miners of Durham 'As a tribute to his long and self sacrificing labours in the cause of Human progress'.

There were many banners swathed in black for the 1873 Big Meeting, the month after his death. Tommy's portrait appeared on the new banners of Bowden Close, Cold Knott, Edmondsley, Inkerman, Thrislington and South Moor. He continued to be a popular figure for many years. He is among the three men pictured on the Haswell Plough banner of 1893 now hanging in Durham Cathedral.

Bibliography

The primary sources of Tommy Ramsey's life are few. Most descriptions of him, such as Harold Heslop's character of the real Tommy in his historical novel *The Earth Beneath*, pp. 96–100, seem to be based on Dr. John Wilson *A History of the Durham Miners' Association 1870–1904*, Veitch & Sons, 1907, pp. 13, 25, 40–41. Dr. Wilson doubtlessly used the Red Hills minutes but some of these are missing for the years 1869–73.

Durham City and County News, 18 August 1871, p.8; and 21 June 1872, p.2.

Durham County Advertiser, 21 June 1872, p.3.

Durham Chronicle, 16 May 1873.

Weekly Chronicle, 10 May 1873 (re-printed in cutting from unknown paper c. 1883)

The Bulletin of the Urban District Council of Blaydon, No. 10, October 1966.

Moira Rutherford

Sir Robert Ropner (1838–1924)   Industrialist

R obert Ropner – shipping merchant, coal exporter, shipbuilder, politician
and philanthropist – was born in Magdeburg in Prussia in 1838. His
father, an army officer, and his mother died of cholera in 1848. Inspired by
stories of the sea, he went to Hamburg at 18 to join the merchant service, but
found he could not stand rough seas. He arrived in West Hartlepool, a
seasick stowaway and a foreigner with little English and little money. He
worked first in a bakery near the docks, married a baker's daughter and in
1859 became a junior clerk to a local colliery fitter and coal exporter. This
was at a time when the Baltic timber and Durham coal trade was flourishing,
and when wooden sailing ships were giving way to iron steamships. West
Dock had been opened in 1847, and no doubt Ralph Ward Jackson's
improvements to the port of West Hartlepool were to be fortuitously
beneficial for the hard-working young newcomer.

In 1860 Ropner was invited to join Thomas Appleby's firm, coal
exporters and colliery agents, to expand its trade. In the following year he
was naturalised and in 1866 became a full partner in the firm which then
became Appleby, Ropner and Co. In 1868 his first custom-built ship, a
steamer with sail, was built by shipbuilders Denton Gray.

Ropner set up on his own in 1875 as R. Ropner and Co. and soon had
the biggest fleet of steamers in West Hartlepool. At first the firm chartered
steamers, but later became shipowners. In the 1880s, Ropner began to build
up the largest tramp steamer company in Britain and the world, with iron
steamships for larger and faster bulk carrying, trading with Europe and the
newer markets of Australia and North and South America, and supplying
British coal to bunkering stations on world trading routes. Ropner was a
pioneer of the cargo-tramp, a type of steamer which was the basis of world
trade until supplanted by liners.

In 1888 Robert bought the shipbuilding yard of Pearse Lockwood and
Co. at Stockton, and renamed it Ropner and Son, Shipbuilders. It used
marine engines made by the adjacent firm, Blair and Co.. Ropner and Son
produced around 60 ships before the outbreak of the First World War, and
also built for other shipowners. It had become by 1895 the third largest
shipyard in Britain. In that year, Ropner patented a new model, the trunk
steamer, which became popular. By 1903, however, Robert Ropner handed
over the business to his sons, John and William, and concerned himself in
Stockton matters and in wider shipping interests. In 1915 the business took
the name Sir R. Ropner and Co. Ltd. The shipyard was sold off to a
syndicate of shipowners in 1919.

The bulk of world trade continued to be carried by cargo-tramp steamers, the "ocean tramps". Ropner's shipping business survived the two world wars and several deep economic depressions. Its part in these wars earned it the nickname "Ropner's Navy". Continued by the third and fourth generations of the family, it went on to diversify into new technology as Ropner plc. It still runs a fleet of ships and is still a family-run firm continuing the surname of its founder.

Meanwhile, however, Robert had entered into his long service in public affairs. In 1867 he was elected to his local council, in 1889 to Durham County Council for the South West Stockton Ward, and in 1896 was Deputy Lieutenant and High Sheriff of County Durham. He was also Colonel of the 1st Battalion of the Durham Light Infantry. Robert was Mayor of Stockton in 1893, and became Stockton's first Freeman in 1901. He was elected Stockton's MP from 1900 until retiring in 1910, during which time he was knighted in 1902 for his services to shipping, and created a baronet in 1904. He also served as a member of the Tees Conservancy Commission (1894–1920), Hartlepool Port and Harbour Commission, Hartlepool Shipping Federation and the Chamber of Shipping. He became JP for the North Riding of Yorkshire from 1899.

Robert Ropner has been described as remote and awe-inspiring, somewhat intimidating, ruthless but clever and straight, yet also generous with a quality of humanity, and he was patriotic, having a warm affection for his adopted country and region. He made great wealth, and in 1881 bought the Preston Hall estate. The mansion there which was his home is now Stockton Art Gallery and Museum. In 1890 he gave 36 acres of land along Hartburn Lane for a public park, developed by the Town Council as Ropner Park, and in 1897 gave the workmen of Stockton and Thornaby a Convalescent Home at Middleton St. George in commemoration of Queen Victoria's Diamond Jubilee.

Bibliography

Ian Dear, *The Ropner Story*, Hutchinson-Benham Ltd., 1986.

James Jamieson, *Durham at the Opening of the Twentieth Century*, edited by W. T. Pike, 1906.

William Page, (editor), *The Victoria History of the Counties of England*, Vol. II, *A History of Durham*, 1907.

Tom Sowler, *A History of the Town and Borough of Stockton-on-Tees*, Teesside Museums and Art Galleries Department, 1972.

Vera Chapman

Hannah Harrison Rushford (1887–1965)   **Alderman**

When Alderman Hannah Rushford was awarded the Freedom of the City of Durham on 3 May, 1963 she was only the second woman in a century to be so honoured. Mrs Rushford was a brilliant organiser and for more than 50 years Durham had benefited from her drive and initiative.

She was born in Durham and went to Lancashire for her first post working on a newspaper. She came back to Durham to establish a needlework shop which she ran for three years until her marriage to Frank Rushford, a journalist who later became editor of Durham County Advertiser Series. During the First World War she served with Colonels Burdon and Blackett in the formation of Durham County Volunteer Regiment and for the next 13 years developed her organising skills as secretary to Bishop Welldon, who was Dean of Durham from 1918–33.

H. H. Rushford, from a photograph published in
'Durham Ladies Lecture Club' magazine, 1969

In 1922 she was presented with the Gold Service badge by the late Lord Baden-Powell after organising a bazaar in the Covered Market which raised £1,200 for the County Scouts Association. She was a founder of the

110

Friends of the Hospital and largely responsible for raising £20,000 for the County Hospital before National Health took over – a ward was called after her. She was also a voluntary prison visitor working with Borstal boys and in 1938 became a justice of the peace and later, chairman of the City Bench.

In 1945 she was the first woman to be elected to the city council and in 1950 became Durham's first woman Mayor. She broke tradition again by appointing six Mayoresses, two, widows of former City Councillors who may have become Mayors if they had lived, while the remainder were representatives of women's organisations with which she was associated – Durham branches of the Business and Professional Women's Club, the Soroptimists Club, the National Council of Women and the Ladies Lecture Club.

The 500 members of the Lecture Club of which she was a founder member in 1939 and presided over until her death, bought her a gold braided, three cornered hat of office. The club was started to bring outstanding speakers so women could obtain first hand knowledge of current topics of interest.

A small committee from the club led by Mrs Rushford raised money to establish and support Mayland Lea, a retirement home for the elderly until it became self supporting.

She was also a county councillor, governor of many schools in the city and chaired several charitable organisations.

When she was made an O.B.E. in the 1964 New Years Honours List, it was for her services in the Durham area for the Ministry of Labour and on the Disablement Advisory Committee.

She and her husband lived for more than fifty years at Grey Tower on the North Road. They had one son who was also a journalist.

Bibliography

Durham County Advertiser, 26 May 1950; 8 March and 3 May 1963; 3 January and 13 March 1964; 10 December 1965.

Durham Ladies' Lecture Tea Club programmes, cuttings and photographs preserved by the late Mrs. E. M. Phillips.

Moira Rutherford

William Scaife (1853–1913)   Durham coal miner and US miners' leader

S caife was born in Witton-le-Wear. His widowed mother raised five children by fieldwork and the mangle. Her remarriage allowed William Scaife to stay at school until he was 12 when he became a miner. He joined the Durham Miners' Association (DMA) as a half-member and at 21 was secretary of the local branch. In 1874 he married Hannah Bromley (who was born in Evenwood). They set up home at Sunniside, by Crook. He worked as a miner at one of the Pease pits, Wooley Colliery, and was elected the checkweighman there. In the autumn of 1881 he emigrated to the United States, with his wife and three daughters, aged five, two and under one year of age. There was then an emigration fever among miners in the county, chiefly directed to the United States and above all, to the Illinois coalfield. The county strike of 1879 brought many to leave, at which time a newspaper observed the fare from New York to Illinois was over £3. During 1880 there was a lull but during 1881, the year of Scaife's emigration, there was a marked revival of the "exodus". An article reviewing the industry during 1881, said it was a year of slow but gradual improvement and "pretty regular employment" but attracted by higher wages "and the golden prospects held out to them", the mining population decreased by between 2,000 and 3,000 (between 3% and 4.5% of the 65,515 coal miners in Durham in 1881) who took their wives and children with them overseas. Newspaper reports show them going in "batches" from distinct localities and thus in association with neighbours and fellow workers. Therefore it seems likely that Scaife owed the beginnings of a successful career in the American union movement not only to his own energy and previous experience as an official but also to his links with a substantial core of former Durham miners. He was to become a member of the executive of the United Mine Workers of America which included at least one other former Durham miner and DMA activist, W. R. Fairley of Alabama, formerly of Monkwearmouth.

Scaife first settled and worked as a miner in Braidwood, Illinois. In 1883 he moved to Coal City and helped Dan McLaughlin in organising the local union, of which he became an officer. From 1887 he was active in the National Federation of Miners and Mine Laborers and in its successor from 1888, the National Progressive Union of Miners and Miner Laborers. At the annual convention of the Illinois miners in 1889 he was elected secretary-treasurer for the state, of district no.12 of the National Progressive Union. He distinguished himself by his conduct of a six month strike of 15,000 men in the northern coalfield of Illinois against wage reduction. In 1890 he helped form the UMWA, was elected to the national executive and was unanimously elected state president of the union. In 1890 he was also elected in the 17th district to the Illinois legislature as a Republican where he served from 1891 to 1893 and promoted bills for mining safety. In 1891 he was appointed a member of the Illinois mining board of examiners which certified mine managers. From 1897 he worked in the Illinois bureau of the Labour Office until 1908 when he became editor (1908–11) of the *Mineworkers Journal*. He was also president (1902–5) and secretary-treasurer (1906–7) of the Mine Managers' and Assistants' Mutual Aid Association. Scaife appears to fit the description "respectable" in that he continued active in the UMWA leadership after the depression of 1893–7 and the failure of Populism eliminated the radicals. In 1904 he was a guest at the Durham Miners' Gala. He was considered a "walking budget" on affairs of the British and the US mining industry.

Bibliography

Roy Andrew, *A History of the Coal Miners of the United States*, (1907), 3rd edition.

Information and advice from:

Howell Harris of Durham University;

Peter Albert of the University of Maryland;

Raymond Collins, Illinois State Library;

Angie Cooper, Coal City Public Library, Illinois;

Alice Dingee, Grundy Co. Genealogical Society, Wilmington, Illinois;

Jane Ehrenhart, Illinois State Historical Library;

Michael Pierce of Ohio State University;

Deborah Steffes, Morris Public Library, Illinois;

Caroline Waldron of the University of Illinois;

Durham Chronicle, 2 May 1879; 30 December 1881; 1 April 1910; 22 April 1910; 6 May 1910.

H. J. Smith

Sir Walter Scott (1771–1832)   **Poet and novelist**

In 1809 Walter Scott visited J. B. S. Morritt, Esq. of Rokeby Hall, which stands near the confluence of the River Tees and River Greta ('The Meeting of the Waters'). Rokeby was in Yorkshire then, but is now in Durham county. Scott was enchanted by the surrounding area, explored it keenly and made notes on what he saw. This resulted in his long narrative poem, *Rokeby* (published in 1813), set in the seventeenth century but more notable for its scenic descriptions. Many of the detailed scenes are in Yorkshire but Durham county references are numerous. The story begins with a guard on night-duty on the round tower of Barnard Castle, and Scott gives an impression of the castle before it became ruined. (The author, despite his care, commits an anachronism here: the poem is set in 1644, but the dilapidation of the castle began a decade earlier.)

Barnard Castle, from a photo by Alan Wilkinson. 'High-crowned he sits, in dawning pale, / The Sovereign of the lovely vale ('Rokeby' – Sir Walter Scott)

In the second Canto, dawn breaks over Durham county:

> The thin grey clouds wax dimly light
> On Brustleton and Houghton height

and the view of Teesdale expands to include the gorge through which the Tees rushes, two miles downstream from the castle,

> Condemn'd to mine a channelled way
> O'er solid sheets of marble grey.

The scene is now best viewed from the Abbey Bridge, built by Mr. Morritt in 1773 and no doubt used by Scott as a viewpoint.

Features seen in the growing light include

> Barnard's bridge of stately stone

and

> Staindrop, who, from her silvan bowers,
> Salutes proud Raby's battled towers.

In Canto III a remorseful brigand remembers his innocent youthful days:

> The cottage, once his sire's, he sees
> Embower'd upon the banks of Tees;
> He views sweet Winston's woodland scene,
> And shares the dance on Gainford-green.

Scott also includes less accessible parts of the dale

> Where Tees in tumult leaves his source
> Thundering o'er Caldron and High Force.

Scott had a significant and direct impact on tourism in Teesdale. Readers wished to visit the scenes which were described in *Rokeby* and which were later illustrated by engravings from paintings by Turner. In 1877 two tourists published a book called *Rambles in Teesdale* in which they followed in Sir Walter's footsteps, frequently quoting from *Rokeby*. Scott continued to be a point of reference in the guide books which began to appear; one such book in the early twentieth century included in its sixty pages nineteen quotations from *Rokeby*.

In 1817 Scott published *Harold the Dauntless*. It, too, includes references to various parts of the county. In Canto I Monkwearmouth is mentioned as part of the lands of the Bishop of Durham; other references include Stanhope, Rookhope, and the River Ganlesse (sic), in Canto II and lively incidents take place in Durham itself, at various points in the poem. In his Introduction of 1830 to *The Lord of the Isles* (first published in 1815), Scott looks back on *Harold the Dauntless* as a 'trifle' and a 'fugitive poem'. Nevertheless, some of its lines have acquired lasting fame and are inscribed on Prebends' Bridge in Durham:

Grey towers of Durham ...
Yet well I love thy mixed and massy piles
Half church of God, half castle 'gainst the Scot,
And long to roam these venerable aisles,
With records stored of deeds long since forgot.

Canto III

Sir Walter himself dined in Durham Castle. He was invited by Lord and Lady Ravensworth to meet the Duke of Wellington at their castle near Durham, and they all attended a banquet held on 3 October 1827 in the old baronial hall in the Bishop's Castle. During the evening Scott's health was proposed by Bishop Van Mildert.

Bibliography

Anon, *Rambles in Teesdale*, 1877.

J. G. Lockhart, *Narrative of the Life of Sir Walter Scott*, 1848.

Alan Wilkinson

Sir Charles Walter Starmer, 1870–1933   Businessman and politician

Starmer was born in Lincolnshire on 12 July 1870, but moved to Loftus, East Cleveland, when very young. He left school at 13 and did a variety of jobs until 1897 when he was advertising representative at *The Northern Echo's* Hartlepool office. He moved to head office in 1902 and became secretary of the Darlington Liberal Association. In 1903, he was elected to Darlington Town Council, and when the *Echo's* proprietor E. D. Walker intimated that he wanted to sell the loss-making paper, it fell to Starmer to negotiate the sale to the Rowntree family of York. In return, Starmer became general manager of the new North of England Newspaper Company. Around the *Echo*, he built a stable of local newspapers – *South Durham and Auckland Chronicle*, *South Durham and Cleveland Mercury*, *Yorkshire Gazette*, *Malton Gazette*, *Auckland Times and Herald*, *Stanley News*, the *Durham County Advertiser*, the *Durham Chronicle*, and the *Northern Despatch*. He also bought papers in Sheffield, Birmingham, Bradford, Nottingham, Lincolnshire, Derbyshire and Lancashire. In 1920, Rowntrees sold "the Starmer Group" to the Pearson family to form the Westminster Press group, of which Starmer became general manager in charge of 40 newspapers selling over one million copies a day across the country. He

116

pioneered many newspaper sales techniques on *The Northern Echo* – like reader insurance, free gifts and a children's club called the Nig Nog Club – which took sales from 5,000 a day in 1903 to 100,000 in 1929. He was knighted in 1917. He stood unsuccessfully for Parliament in 1918 in Sedgefield, won the Cleveland seat in 1923 but lost it in 1924. He was also unsuccessful in Cleveland in the 1929 Election. He was twice mayor of Darlington, and in his second spell in 1933 opened the Darlington Memorial Hospital with Prince George, the Duke of Kent. He lived in Danby Lodge, Coniscliffe Road, Darlington, but died suddenly at his Westminster residence on 27 June 1933.

Bibliography

Chris Lloyd, *Attacking the Devil: 130 Years of The Northern Echo*, *The Northern Echo*, 1999.

Chris Lloyd

William Thomas Stead, 1849–1912   Journalist and Moral Campaigner

William Thomas Stead was acclaimed by Matthew Arnold as the founder of "new journalism" – he introduced the interview, the investigation, sensationalism and typographical design to newspapers. Born in 1849 at Embleton near Alnwick in Northumberland, he was educated at home by his father, a Congregational minister, until 11. He finished his education at a Congregational school near Wakefield and in 1863 he became clerk and later speechwriter to Charles Smith, a Newcastle councillor and Russian vice-consul. In 1870, he began writing articles for the newly-founded halfpenny Liberal paper in Darlington, *The Northern Echo*, and in 1871, with no other newspaper experience, was appointed its editor. In 1876 he began campaigning against the Bulgarian Atrocities being committed by the Turkish Empire. Fire and brimstone articles inflamed the North East and re-awoke the political spirit of W. E. Gladstone who said: "It is a sincere regret to me that I cannot read more of the *Echo*, for to read the *Echo* is to dispense with the necessity of reading other papers. It is admirably got up in every way." The first session of the United Parliaments of Bulgaria and Eastern Roumelia passed a unanimous vote of thanks to the *Echo* for stirring European opinion. In 1880, Stead left Darlington to become editor of the influential Liberal paper the *Pall Mall Gazette*, London, where in 1885 he launched his Maiden Tribute of Modern Babylon crusade against child prostitution. This was important in raising the age of consent raised from 13 to 16 but as part of his campaign he procured a 13-year-old girl for £5 from her mother and placed her in a brothel where he became her first customer. He chloroformed her and spirited her away to France for five weeks while he published her story in the *Gazette* under sensationalist headlines like "The confessions of a brothel keeper" and "Strapping girls down". This resulted in his being sentenced to nine weeks, including three days hard labour, in Holloway Prison for abduction. He went on to edit the *Review of Reviews* in London, but in later life became very interested in Spiritualism to which he had been converted while in Darlington. In 1912, against the advice of a clairvoyant, he set sail aboard the *Titanic* for New York to attend a peace conference and to persuade "a famous direct voice medium" to return with him to England. On 14 April, the *Titanic* hit an iceberg and Stead went down playing bridge. He was probably the most famous Englishman aboard. Ironically, throughout his career, Stead had featured stories about sinking liners and one of the more remarkable tales that he published in the *Pall Mall Gazette* was that of the sole survivor of such a disaster.

W. T. Stead, 1912

His prescient editorial comment ended: "This is exactly what might take place if liners are sent to sea short of boats." There are wall plaques in his memory in Wallsend and Central Park, New York. Opposite *The Northern Echo* offices in Darlington is the stone from his house where he tethered his pony and dogs. The Inscription reads: "The boulder is a fitting symbol of his indomitable courage and strength of character."

Bibliography

Victor Pierre Jones, *W. T. Stead: Saint or Sensationalist*, Gooday Publishing, 1988.

Chris Lloyd, *Attacking the Devil: 130 Years of The Northern Echo*, The Northern Echo, 1999.

Chris Lloyd

Norman Sunderland, BA (1909–1982)   Historian

A professional historian and teacher, Norman Sunderland spent all his working life in Darlington. After his retirement in 1970 he continued to apply his expertise in local history, devotedly researching and writing until his death in 1982.

Norman Sunderland came from the village of Methley, near Leeds, and graduated with an honours degree in history at the University of Manchester in 1930, followed by a Teacher's Diploma in 1931. That year, he was appointed master at the Grammar School of Queen Elizabeth in Darlington at a time when it was difficult for graduates to get posts in secondary schools. After a break for War Service in which he was seconded to the American Army and awarded the American Bronze Star, he resumed his career at the school, becoming Head of History, Deputy Head and Headmaster.

He had been accepted in 1955 to do an M.A. thesis at Manchester University on the history of his school, but this became instead a book, *The History of the Free Grammar School of Queen Elizabeth, Darlington*, published in 1963 on the 400th anniversary of the granting of its Charter and in honour of the visit to the school of H. M. Queen Elizabeth the Queen Mother.

In 1960, Norman had become founder Chairman of Darlington Historical Society. He encouraged members to be active, and memorable exhibitions were mounted in 1965 for the town's County Borough Golden Jubilee and in 1967 for the Centenary of the Borough Charter of Incorporation. Members wrote a booklet *Darlington in 1915* for the Golden Jubilee. To mark the Centenary, the Society, with help from the Borough Council, published Norman Sunderland's *A History of Darlington*, of which a leather-bound volume was presented to H. M. Queen Elizabeth II on her visit to the town's celebrations.

The 1960s were a time when demolition and renewal were fashionable. With the Historical Society's backing, Norman was instrumental in saving the attractive rear wall of the Nag's Head inn, the only remaining Tudor building in the town centre. The Tudor period was Norman Sunderland's chief interest. This bore fruit as two volumes in Durham County Library Local History Publications series, *Tudor Darlington*, Part I, (1974) and Part II, (1976).

N. Sunderland, photo courtesy of *The Northern Echo*

Through his vigilance at sales, he bought and donated numerous documents, paintings and printed matter to the town's archives at the

Borough Library and to the later County Record Office and the University of Durham Department of Palaeography and Diplomatic, now the Archives and Special Collections. He rescued, for example, the local copies of the Tithe Awards of Darlington and Blackwell, and most notably, the Borough Books 1612-1633, the record of proceedings of the Bishop of Durham's manorial court in Darlington from which he was able to depict life in the town in the 17th century.

Between 1960 and 1965 Norman wrote some eighty or so detailed but readable and often humorous articles in the *Northern Despatch* covering a wide range of incidents in the life of the town. These were based on contemporary materials, carefully explained and placed in the context of their times and of the nation.

Norman Sunderland made a valuable contribution to the northern region at a period when local history was in the early stages of its rise to the wide popularity it now enjoys. He set a scholarly standard for others to follow, and was ever ready to help them to do so. A modest, generous man, he was concerned above all with the lives of ordinary people past and present.

Bibliography

Vera Chapman, 'Norman Sunderland, 1909–1982', *Durham County Local History Society Bulletin*, 29, December 1982.

Darlington and Stockton Times, 15 May 1982.

F. M. Layfield, 'List of Donations by N. Sunderland', *Darlington Branch Librarian*, 1 July 1982.

Northern Echo, 12 May 1982.

Vera Chapman

Sir Henry Taylor (1800–86)   **Senior Civil Servant, Author, Poet and Dramatist**

S ir Henry Taylor was born at Bishop Middleham on 18 October 1800, the youngest of three sons of George Taylor and his wife Eleanor (née Ashworth). His family subsequently moved to St. Helen Auckland, then to Witton le Wear. In 1814 he was midshipman on *HMS Elephant* under Captain Francis W. Austen. He was appointed to a government clerkship in 1816, under the patronage of Charles Arbuthnot, friend of the Duke of

Wellington. He was in Barbados for a brief period in 1820. From here he returned to Witton Hall, Witton le Wear, where he did most of his early writing. His first article was published in the *Quarterly Review* in 1822. The countryside surrounding Witton Hall was the inspiration for and perpetuated in some of of his pastoral verse.

Sir Henry Taylor, from a photograph by Mr Hawker of Bournemouth

He entered the Colonial Office in 1824 with the aid of Sir Henry Holland and remained there for the remainder of his career but shunned promotion to senior posts, including the Governorship of Canada and the post of Under Secretary of State for the Colonies, to spend more time on his literary works. He was a notable supporter of the policy of 'melioration', rather than abolition of slavery. Following the success of his drama, *Philip van Artevelde*, in 1834, he became the toast of London society. He married Alice Spring Rice, daughter of Thomas Spring Rice, first Baron Monteagle in 1839. A popular figure in London circles, he counted among his friends

William Gladstone, the third Earl Grey, Tennyson, Wordsworth, Thackeray and Robert Southey. His literary works included *Isaac Comnenus* (1828), *The Statesman* (1836), *Edwin the Fair* (1842), *The Eve of the Conquest and other poems* (1847), *The Virgin Widow* (1850), and *St. Clements Eve* (1862). He was awarded the Order of St. Michael and St. George for services to the Colonial Office in 1869.

Bibliography

Henry L. Hall, *The Colonial Office: a History*, London & New York, 1937.

H. Taylor, *Autobiography of Henry Taylor*, volumes 1 & 2, London, 1885.

D. M. Young, *The Colonial Office in the Early Nineteenth Century*, Plymouth, 1961.

Grey Papers (3rd Earl), University of Durham.

Taylor Papers, Bodleian Library, University of Oxford.

Margaret Ray

Christopher Tennant (c. 1780–1839)   Entrepreneur

Christopher Tennant is credited in W. W. Tomlinson's *History of the North Eastern Railway* with being the promoter of the Clarence railway, the Hartlepool Dock and Railway Company, the Hartlepool Junction Company and what became the Stockton and Hartlepool Railway Company, as well as the thwarted South West and South Durham Railway schemes.

Yet possibly because his role was promotional rather than managerial his place in the early industrial development of the South Durham coalfield has been largely ignored by more recent historians.

One reason for this may be that he has left very little direct documentary evidence of his activities.The letters and references that survive are embedded in the correspondence of others or in company management minute books .

Tennant was born inYarm, probably at the end of 1780 or the beginning of 1781. Nothing is known of his family background; but his brother Thomas, five or six years his junior became a very prosperous sailcloth and rope manufacturer in Stockton and possibly this was a family business. It was Thomas rather than Christopher who became the investor in most of the various enterprises with which the older man was associated.

Christopher reputedly saw service in the Royal Navy; but by 1818 when he funded an independent survey of a possible route for a canal from the Auckland coalfield to Teesside his main source of income seems to have been from his lime kilns at East Thickley near Shildon. The proposed canal was to be the means of achieving cheaper bulk west to east mineral carriage to serve this, and other interests including possible coastwise coal shipment from the Tees to the East coast and London markets.

C. Tennant, courtesy of Brian Mills of the International Bond and Share Society

In the debates that followed , which are covered in detail in Tomlinson, Tennant became the spokesman for the Stockton shipping interest and it was as such, when it became clear that the Stockton and Darlington promoters did not intend to enter the coastwise coal trade, that he found himself forced to revive a rail line version of his canal scheme. But despite considerable London and Stockton backing and Tennant's best efforts at lobbying, the revived scheme, the Tees and Weardale Railway, failed to get sufficient support for parliamentary approval; and within months of the Stockton and Darlington railway's opening, its directors found themselves compelled by financial pressures to go back on the decision that had alienated Tennant and his backers, and to enter the London trade.

Intent on retaining a monopoly of what proved to be a very lucrative operation the Stockton and Darlington directors refused Tennant's proffered collaboration in developing improved shipping facilities on the Tees and drove him to promote a totally separate company, the Clarence, which got parliamentary sanction on a wave of anti-monopolist free trade enthusiasm in 1828 .

It may have been the acquisition of the coal royalty of Coxhoe by one of the leading shareholders of the Clarence that led Tennant, while the Clarence was under construction to turn his attention towards the latest scheme to revive the decayed harbour of Hartlepool as a coal port. The project had the backing of the largely non-resident oligarchy that constituted the corporation of the town and of a number of prestigious Durham City professional men; some of them also members of a partnership developing the nearby coal royalty at Thornley. Tennant appears to have been approached initially because of his experience in shepherding bills of incorporation through parliament but he was subsequently employed as the 'on the spot' supervisor of the engineering work. His motivation for moving to Hartlepool may have been primarily financial for although his brother became a substantial shareholder he himself took no shares in the company.

In 1834 the newly opened Clarence was experiencing the same problems of accumulated debt incurred during construction, delays in building up traffic and inexperienced management, as many other early railways, and had also to contend with the outright hostility of the Stockton and Darlington and the still entrenched monopoly of the North East's coal owning establishment.

It was in the hope of building up traffic, and with the backing of a number of local interested parties, that in October 1835 Tennant made the first proposals for what was in effect a revised version of the Tees and Weardale scheme of the early 1820s, which would use one of the branches of the Clarence to carry limestone out of Weardale, and coal from collieries currently being developed, with the option of shipment either from the Tees or via a still to be launched link line to the rail and harbour development at Hartlepool. Although Tennant and his brother had retained a stake in the Clarence there was some understandable initial disquiet among the directors that this development would take traffic from the company's main line and its coaling facilities at Port Clarence. So by early December 1835 two lines were envisaged, to link up to the two westward spurs of the Clarence, one with a strong element of co-shareholding with the Hartlepool company, the other comparably financially related to the Clarence.

These two schemes, the South Durham and the South West Durham were brought before parliament by Tennant in the spring and summer of 1836, at a time of nationwide railway speculation and free market propaganda. Profiting from this and in cooperation with the London end of the coal trade, a group, of which Tennant was a prominent member, was successful in forcing the repeal of the archaic legislation that had thus far prevented the formation of joint stock mining companies, but the promoters failed to get either of the railway bills through parliament as a result of the combined opposition of Stockton and Darlington supporters and the North Eastern coal trade establishment.

During the debates public confidence in the Clarence had been deliberately undermined by revelations about its financial problems and Tennant himself was the victim of personal abuse as 'that notorious projector and tramping quack'. The outcome of this bruising sequence of events was a series of complex negotiations in which if not the initiator Tennant was clearly involved, to link the financing of the Byers Green branch of the Clarence and its westward extension, to that of the joint stock coal company whose protagonists had been involved in the anti monopolist agitation and the success of whose venture depended upon effective rail links.

At the same time shareholders in the Hartlepool Dock and Railway company also launched a subsidiary company to complete the link between their existing short length of railway and the Byers Green branch of the Clarence. There is no diirect evidence that Tennant was the initiator of this scheme which although a logical development would inevitably take traffic away from the Clarence's main line and the company staithes at Port Clarence; and indeed it was opposed by the main body of the Clarence directorate which tried to prevent its completion.

But Tennant with a commitment to the prosperity of both companies was more concerned at the slow progress on the construction of the Byers

Green branch and the failure of the coal company to open the collieries that were supposed to be going to serve it and it was in this situation that, at the end of 1838, in collaboration with several major Clarence shareholders and the company's newly appointed solicitor Ralph Ward Jackson, he initiated a proposal for a non-parliamentary link line between the main line of the Clarence and the south side of the harbour at Hartlepool. Once again although Tennant was the initiator of the project he was not a shareholder or a member of the provisional committee of what became the Stockton and Hartlepool junction railway, but was paid for his services.

Nor did he have time to see the line come into operation, for on 12 September 1839 while engaged on what may have been a related project, to supply fish from Hartlepool by rail to the interior of the country, he was suddenly taken ill and died.

He was buried in the churchyard of St Hilda's in Hartlepool. There is no evidence that he ever married and during his time in Hartlepool he seems to have lived with his widowed mother who predeceased him by only one year and is also buried there. His younger brother died in 1840 leaving a fortune of nearly £25,000.

Christopher Tennant remains difficult to categorise. Apart from the spiteful attacks on him in 1836 he seems to have been well respected by his business contemporaries who valued his hard won expertise in company promotion , but in north eastern history he is remembered primarily as the promoter of the Clarence, the less successful rival to the Stockton and Darlington. This perception has both diminished appreciation of his real contribution to the complex beginnings of the industrial development of South Durham and exaggerated the scale of his individual role in both the chequered history of the Clarence and the development of the Port of Hartlepool.

Bibliography

Chaytor Papers, North Yorkshire County Record Office.

Guildhall Library, London, 'Coal-trade scrapbook 1800–1840.'

Hansard's Parliamentary Debates, 3rd series, 33, House of Lords, 3 May 1936, 511–4 and 35, 11 and 15 July 1836, 60, 225–7.

Hartlepool Local Studies Library printed list of subscribers to the Hartlepool Dock and Railway Co., Borthwick Institute York, The will of Thomas Allison Tennant dated 1837 provides for an annuity for his mother and brother which suggests that Christopher was not a wealthy man.

M. W. Kirby, *The Origins of Railway Enterprisse – The Stockton and Darlington Railway 1821–1863*, pp. 50, 71, 72, CUP, 1993.

Parish Register, Yarm, St. Mary Magdalen, 1781 and 1786, Cleveland Record Office.

W. Parson, and W. White, *History, Directory and Gazetteer of the Counties of Durham and Northumberland 1827–8*, vol. 1, p. 319, vol. 2, p. 209.

Public Record Office, Kew, Rail 117/4, Clarence Railway management committee minutes, July–August 1836, December 1836, Rail 117/1, General meeting of Clarence shareholders, 22 November 1838, Rail 668/20, Stockton and Hartlepool Railway Co. Journal.

R. Smith, *Sea Coal for London:the history of the Coal Factors in the London Market*, p. 244, London, 1961.

W. Stokes, 'Regional finance and the definition of a financial region' in Royle, E., (editor), *Issues of Regional Identity*, pp. 134–6, MUP, 1998.

W. Stokes, 'The Joint Stock Generation', pp. 2–23, Durham County Local History Society *Bulletin*, 55, 1996.

W. W. Tomlinson, *The North Eastern Railway: Its Rise and Development*, p. 170, 1915, reprint 1967.

Winifred Stokes

John Todd (1840–1899)   Sea captain

Only a few 19th century sea captains tried to set down their experiences of a working life that varied from the boring to the terrifying, and which was the most dangerous of all the major occupations of the industrial world. Captain John Todd of Sunderland was one of those exceptional men. Born in 1840, he was at sea from 1855 until his death in 1899, when he went down with his ship off Beachy Head. In his time he experienced everything such a sailor could, carrying cargoes as ordinary as coal and as exotic as opium for employers as different as the Earl of Durham and the Governor-General of Asiatic Turkey. He fought pirates and mutineers, was wrecked and stranded, wrote poetry, and from sea and land poured out letters to the press on everything from industrial relations to art. He also somehow found time to write a book on seamanship, a life of Sunderland's naval hero, Jack

Crawford, and to do oil paintings of shipMuch of the information in this biography comes from his unpublished autobiography in two manuscript volumes of four hundred pages each. The originals were found a few years ago under the stairs of an old house in Sunderland along with a number of cuttings of Todd's letters to the papers and some relating to his death, a few printed copies of his poems and a bundle of family photographs. Over five months in 1886 two quality quarto notebooks bought from Hill's of Sunderland were each filled to the last line of the last page.

Todd came from a more well-to-do background than most nineteenth century sea captains. His grandfather owned a wharf on the Thames and his father was fitter (shipping agent) to the Lambton Estate. From seven to thirteen Todd was at boarding school, the last three years in London, at a school where "... Young Gentlemen are prepared for the Oxford, Cambridge, and other Public Examinations, or other Professional and Mercantile Pursuits."

John Todd, from a photograph supplied by George Patterson

In 1854 at the age of 14 he ran away to Liverpool to go to sea. He failed, but was apprenticed to a Sunderland captain a year later. Badly treated and almost killed on his first voyage to Burma his indentures were cancelled when he came home. Three months later he went to sea again but this time as an ordinary seaman, starting on 17 years of wandering the world. On his periodic home stays he passed his officer's exams and eventually returned to Sunderland, married and settled into more routine seafaring work on the Lambton steamers. Although he had an education and became an officer Todd also served before the mast as an ordinary seaman so he wrote with authority of the hardships, rivalries and pleasures, often illicit, of the ordinary seafarer.

Between 1855 and 1862 Todd's voyages took him all over the world. In the course of his wanderings he experienced hurricanes, icebergs and an earthquake, was stabbed, rescued from a shark and twice left ships which were lost with all hands on their next voyage. In its next phase his career included attacks by natives in Queensland, a cannibal feast in New Guinea and a narrow escape from pirates off Bali. He went to Calcutta and spent three months without a ship, learning Hindustanee in the meantime. He sailed as mate to Cochin and just escaped with his life in a mutiny by the native crew. In India he joined the Bombay Marine, troop carrying for the government, then two years later returned to Sunderland, passed his master's ticket and sailed as chief mate for Ceylon. The captain was drunk, the crew mutinied and beat Todd up and left him in St. Helena. He shipped next to Cape Town, spent three months as a rigger there, becoming engaged to Polly, then signed on for a coastal voyage which turned out instead to be for Mauritius. Offered command of the ship, Todd forgot Polly and sailed for China. At Singapore the vessel was grossly overloaded and Todd left the ship which was lost when she sailed.

He went back to Bombay and signed on as chief officer then captain (at a massive £40 a month) on a ship smuggling opium. A year of that and Todd sailed a sinking ship from Karachi to the Persian Gulf to become master of the yacht of the Governor General of Baghdad, Midhat Pasha, sailing the Tigris and Euphrates. In 1872 Todd returned to Sunderland and was taken on by the Lambton Company, the end of his roving days symbolised by his marriage to Mary Rutledge, sister of a fellow officer. From then until 1899 Todd made the regular runs from Sunderland with coal to the French Atlantic coast, then ballast to Huelva in northern Spain and back to the North East with iron ore, no longer sailing in rotten wooden hulks but in well-found steamships.

Settled in Sunderland, he wrote that his wife was as happy as he was except for one thing – "she wants me off the sea", which had already claimed the lives of two of his four brothers, and even of his sister, who committed suicide after being jilted, while Todd himself had lost his ship, *the Heathpool*, in 1884 when he misjudged his ability to navigate in fog off the coast of Brittany.

For fifteen more years Todd safely sailed the same waters, becoming a well-known figure in Sunderland, author of a book on seamanship and regular contributor to the *Sunderland Herald* of Tory views on maritime and local political matters. On 31 March 1899 Todd's ship, the iron steamer *Heathpool II* left Sunderland with a crew of 14 and 200 tons of coal bound for St. Nazaire. Off Beachy Head a dense fog developed and a much larger steamer smashed into the *Heathpool's* starboard side and sank her.

The loss of a ship and eight men which seems so dramatic now was almost routine a hundred years ago. Indeed, the *Sunderland Echo's* headline 'Terrible Disaster in the Channel' referred not to *the Heathpool* but to the wreck of the passenger steamer *Stella* with the loss of more than 80 lives.

John Todd was not a typical seafarer of his time. His life before the mast was one which many a sailor experienced, with the difference that he was able to observe, think and write about it. He tells us of the horrors – the ill-treatment, the danger, the coffin-ships and scurvy, and he describes the pleasures – the achievements, the comradeship, the fun ashore and the sheer adventure of the sea. He was untypical in rising from ordinary seaman to captain, a rise which by his later years was almost unknown. *The Sunderland Herald* tribute said "(he) was a beautiful character, of varied gifts and attainments, loyal to owner and crew, loving his profession and ... a just man of the highest honour." Todd has no memorial of his own but he was a member of the committee which erected the monument to Jack Crawford that still stands in Sunderland's Mowbray Park and serves as a memorial to the whole seafaring tradition.

Bibliography

A longer version of this biography appeared in the Millennium issue of *Sunderland's History* Vol. 9, Journal of Sunderland Antiquarian Society.

J. Todd, *A Sketch of the Life of Jack Crawford*, Sunderland, 1889.

J. Todd, *Practical Seamanship*, 1890.

Todd's Autobiography remains in private hands.

Obituaries in *Merchant Service Review*, 8 April 1899; *Sunderland Herald*, 12 April 1899.

George Patterson

The Revd. Canon Henry Baker Tristram (1822–1906)   Naturalist, Freemason and Churchman

Canon Tristram would have been a familiar sight to many, as he made his way to the Cathedral, robed in a very voluminous surplice which billowed in the wind and wearing his mortar board and LL.D. hood of scarlet cloth and lavender silk. Some would see him walking with Pepper, his daughter's Dandy Dinmont dog, whilst supervising the planting and maintenance of the Banks. Others would be greeted by him as the genial host in welcoming many missionaries, scientists and ornithologists to his home in the College. The Vicar of St. Nicholas' Church said at his funeral the 'people knew him as the intrepid traveller and pioneer, the learned author, the scientific explorer, the distinguished naturalist and the Churchman zealous, frank and untiring ... In Durham he will be known for his 70 years of residence, for his love for our institutions, his fostering care of our natural beauties'. (*The Durham County Advertiser*, 13 March 1903.) Perhaps a century later, the planting of the Banks may be seen as his most lasting legacy to Durham.

He was born on 11 May 1822, at Eglingham, near Alnwick in Northumberland, the first son of Henry Baker Tristram, then Vicar of Eglingham, and Charlotte Jocelyn Smith, both of profound Evangelical principles. His mother had opened and taught in the first girls' school in north Northumberland. After the early deaths of both parents the family moved with their stepmother to Durham where Tristram attended Durham Grammar School and 'became associated with John Hancock, who imbued into him a love of nature and in some measure laid the foundation for his future success as a naturalist'. (*The Durham Chronicle*, 16 March 1906.) Later he became a Governor of the school for thirty years and its Science society became known as the Tristram Society after his death.

In 1839 Tristram gained a scholarship to Lincoln College, Oxford, and graduated with a second class degree in classics. He was ordained deacon in 1845, priest in 1846 and afterwards spent a year's curacy in Morchard Bishop, a scattered country parish in Devonshire where he had to visit parishioners on horseback. However he caught a chill after a long ride in wet

132

weather and largely for health reasons he left Devonshire for a military chaplaincy in Bermuda.

On returning to England Tristram was licensed and inducted to the parish of Castle Eden in 1849. Soon after, he married Eleanor Mary Bowlby, who came from a well-known and established family in Durham. One of her earliest memories was going with her grandmother and aunt to superintend the vaccination of the poor children in Framwellgate. Their marriage was a long and happy one and at Castle Eden they began their family of seven daughters and one son. Their lives were divided between parochial and diocesan duties, and the start of Tristram's regular trips abroad to the Sagara and to Palestine with the consequent authorship of his many scientific observations and discoveries. 1859 saw the establishment of the British Ornithological Union of which Tristram was a founder member, and the publication of the first number of the journal *Ibis*. His paper 'On the Ornithology of Northern Africa' in the first volume was significant in that he showed an early acceptance of the Darwinian theory of evolution and in the fact that it was published a month before *The Origin of the Species*. It could be claimed that he was the first zoologist to apply the theory of natural selection to his work on birds.

Rowland Burdon of Castle Eden and Tristram had been determined to establish a female Training School for Schoolmistresses in Durham, despite strong opposition. They set about fund-raising and finding a suitable site. 'My father used to go up and down the Quay side in Newcastle to interview the merchants and ask for their donations, and was so successful that in a year he had raised £2,500, besides large sums raised by other helpers'. (See Tristram, Louisa H. H. 1898.) The College was founded in 1858 and since 1859 Tristram acted in the capacity of Honorary Secretary of the Management Committee. It was his suggestion that the College adopted the name of St. Hild's in 1898.

In 1860 Tristram became Master of Greatham Hospital and Rector of Greatham which he held until he was offered a residential Canonry in Durham Cathedral in 1873. His first book *The Great Sahara* was published. However his parochial work was not neglected; a problem with drunkenness was solved by closing four public houses and a reading room opened; and during his time the 600th anniversary of the hospital's founding was kept. His daughters remembered 'a strong gale blew the tent down and my father told the men to slope the poles in the teeth of the wind ... the tent weathered the gale and a parishioner was heard to remark "I respect Dr. Tristram from yesterday!" ... the parting gift of the farmers of the parish was the carting of all our furniture the 20 miles to Durham'. (See Tristram, Louisa H. H. 1898, and *The Durham County Advertiser*, 22 August 1952.)

Tristram was to remain at Durham for the rest of his life, and continued his interests in the Penitentiary and as Honorary Chaplain to the Hospital. In 1868 he became a Fellow of the Royal Society and received an Honorary LL.D. of Edinburgh. He had been an active freemason since University days and became a distinguished member, rising to many senior posts, one being the Provincial Grand Master of Mark Masons of Northumberland and Durham. Tristram Lodge, Shildon, was named after him.

The Revd Canon H. B. Tristram, photo taken from a portrait in Durham Masonic Hall

He continued his many travels to different parts of the world, becoming an authority on the flora and fauna of Palestine, and the Palestine Exploration Fund published his extensive research in 1884. Its thoroughness and reliability has stood the test of time as it has been recently used in a survey *The Early Bronze Age Environment of the Southern Jhor and the Moab Plateau* by Jack Harlan, edited by Adnen Hadidi, 1985.

Both his daughter and granddaughter can remember his pride in 'his garden' and in his beloved trees, planted and developed from rubbish heaps and neglected land which skirt the river. In April, 1875, the Dean & Chapter agreed that £20 be expended under the direction of Dr. Tristram in Trees and Shrubs for the Banks and College precincts, and a further £110 to be spent in the following two years. (Dean & Chapter Minutes for 26 March 1875; 3 April 1875; 19 May 1876.) Local people sent him gifts of plants, such as Mr. Le Keux of Saddler Street, who presented two cart-loads of plants and flowers for the purpose of ornamenting the Banks in May 1876. Tristram had actively supported the Tyneside Natural History Society for many years, and had strongly promoted early Acts of Parliament, such as the Wild Bird Protection Bill in 1872. His last letter to the press implored the public to protect the plants, animals and birds, especially the few remaining pairs of Tawny Owls, on the banks of the River Wear. This plea for conservation and protection still lives in the memory of Durham.

Bibliography

Dean & Chapter Minutes of Durham for 26 March 1875; 3 April 1875; 19 May 1876.

Eleanor M. Fleming, 'Recollections of my Grandparents Canon and Mrs. Tristram', Unpublished typed MSS.

Jack R. Harlan, *The Early Bronze Age Environment of the Southern Jhor and the Moab Plateau*, Ed. Adnen Hadidi, Publishing Department of Antiquities of Jordan, 1985.

The Durham Chronicle, 16 March 1906.

The Durham County Advertiser, 13 March 1903; 22 August 1952.

Louisa H. H. Tristram, 'Recollections of Henry Baker Tristram, D.D., F.R.S.', Unpublished typed MSS.

Judith E. T. Tarrant

John Walker (1781–1859)   The Inventor of the Friction Light

John Walker was born on 29 May 1781 at Stockton on Tees where his father was a licensed grocer. His mother – Mary Peacock – was the daughter of the Reverend Thomas Peacock – at that time Curate of Marton in Cleveland.

John was apprenticed to Watson Alcock, a well respected surgeon at Stockton. It was customary in these days for apothecary apprenticeship to start at the age of fourteen or fifteen.

In 1801, Stockton had a population of 3,641 while its fellow port on the Tees – Yarm – had 1,300. Both towns served the prosperous agricultural areas of South Durham and North Yorkshire, trading with East coast ports and the continent.

Stockton was an enterprising community and the new century soon saw two important communication developments. In 1810, the Tees Cut shortened the river transit time to the sea; while the opening in 1825 of the world's first passenger railway was a momentous event in global terms.

The medical profession locally reflected Stockton's progressive commercial life. There were at least five surgeons in active practice serving the town and surrounding country. Alcock was mayor of Stockton in 1807 and 1808. In 1790 Stockton had founded a voluntary Dispensary – the 13th such local provision to relieve the poor. Thus the community into which John Walker came at the start of the 19th century was a progressive commercial centre with an active medical profession.

When he completed his apprenticeship, John left to work in London before returning to serve as an assistant with Alcock. Surprisingly John left medical practice – apparently he found surgical operations disturbing. Considering the barbarity of operations in these pre-anaesthetic days, his horror was not unreasonable. John chose to enter pharmacy and sought training at Durham and York. In June 1819, he returned to Stockton to set up pharmacy in the High Street. His premises were next to well-known booksellers and publishers – Christopher and Jennett.

What knowledge we have of John's discovery is based on one surviving business ledger or day-book. This book has entries for the period 1825 up to 1829. Pharmacists in these days supplied medicines and many other materials to a range of customers – surgeons and apothecaries, businessmen, farmers and sportsmen.

The entries in John's day-book have been meticulously analysed by the late Mrs Doreen Thomas. Her work revealed how his medical and pharmacological background underpinned his wide interests in botany, mineralogy, astronomy and chemistry. In one field in particular, analysis of his ledger reveals his interest in explosive mixtures. He was supplying a paste prepared from potassium chlorate and antimony sulphide for use by local sportsmen in their guns. One of his customers – Mr Cooper – was a gunsmith. On 19 November 1825 he comments on one supply of potassium chlorate and antimony sulphide paste: 'excellent' – suggesting he was experimenting with the ingredients of a percussion powder. While explosive chemicals were known to produce a flame, no one had mastered the step of transferring such energy directly to wood. John may have been working with wooden sticks tipped with his percussion cap paste and had thought to coat wooden sticks with sulphur. Was his concept to transfer flame from paste to the wood?

The story is related that one day, a stick with his explosive paste on its tip, was accidentally scraped against a rough hearthstone. It produced a small explosion and fire, the fire transferred to the wood which caught alight and burned with a flame. John's genius lay in his recognition of the importance of this event. A lesser mind might have noted the event without pursuing its significance. Knowing the constituents of his powder, he could reproduce his experiment precisely. He refined his method to set easily portable wooden sticks alight reliably.

His day-book does not provide any entries to document the period between his discovery and the marketing of his wooden sticks tipped with his special mixture. The entry on Saturday 7 April 1827 is the first to record any sale of his invention:

> to Mr Hixon (a local solicitor)

> "Sulphorata Hyperoxygenata Frict 100," price one shilling with 2 pence for a tin case.

In the left hand corner of this entry, the number 30th has been crossed out and Nº 30 entered.

John has not yet chosen a name for his invention. The next entry in his day-book recording its sale appeared on 7 September 1827 and used the title 'friction lights' for his invention. Mr Fenwick purchased 84 friction lights, costing 10 pence, plus two pence for their tin.

The ledger which ran until 1829, recorded regular sales of his invention to customers not just in Stockton, but across the North of England. John did not patent his invention and does not appear to have tried to make a profit therefrom. Rival 'matches' soon appeared on the market and it is believed that by 1830 or 1831, John ceased to sell his friction lights.

John continued his pharmacy, living quietly with his sisters in Stockton until retiring in 1858. John Walker was described as slight in stature – a smart, trim little man: rather retiring – studious and well read, whose information was large and extensive, and whose conversation was constructive; a walking encyclopaedia, modestly avoiding pretence of superior knowledge; ever enquiring and experimental.

John Walker died at Stockton at Tees on 1 May 1859. He was buried in Norton Parish Churchyard.

His invention of a portable fire-producing stick proved reliable and infinitely more practical than the previous tinder box system. It is surprising if John could have realised the impact of his invention. To take one small example, previously householders 'smoored' their fire overnight to retain its light. Such smooring is commemorated in the lines of an old Scottish prayer:

This night / And every night / Each single night / Amen.

The lines recall the opening of the Lyke Wake Dirge:

This yah neet, this yah neet
Ivvery neet an' all,
Fire and fleet a' cannle leet,
An' Christ tak up thy saul.

Friction matches soon put paid to the need for 'smooring', so that perpetual flames lingering in a few Inns, are museum relics today.

Bibliography

Dictionary of National Biography, volume XV, OUP, 1973.

Gateshead Observer, James Clephan editor, undated reference sited by D. Thomas.

Loudon, I. S. L., 'Origins & Growth of Dispensary Movement in England', *Bulletin* of *History of Medicine*, vol. 1, 55, 322–345, 1981.

Rowlands, J., 'Annals of a Teesside Practice 1793–1969', *Medical History*, pp. 388–403, XVL, 4 October 1972.

Thomas, D., *Strike a Light: John Walker 1781–1859*, 1976 reprint, Cleveland County Council.

G. Stout

Alfred Waterhouse, FRIBA, RA, LL.D. (1830–1905)   Architect

The Victorian architect Alfred Waterhouse was famous in his own time. He did substantial work in the North of England, in County Durham and in Darlington. In practice 1853–1902, his peak period was 1860–1880 when he was recognised as the leading architect in Britain. He and his son Paul and grandson Michael all became Presidents of the Royal Institute of British Architects. Recognised as his best buildings are Manchester Town Hall, 1868, Eaton Hall, Chester, 1870–1883, for the 1st Duke of Westminster, and the Natural History Museum in Kensington, London, 1873–1881.

Waterhouse set up practice in Manchester in 1853. His early commissions came from his Quaker relatives and friends and from winning architectural competitions. His fame as an innovator and a master of practical planning who designed buildings suitable for their purpose, solved problems of difficult sites and kept within costs arose from his Manchester Law Courts, 1859, and continued with Manchester Town Hall, 1868. An accomplished artist and a Royal Academician, his dramatic and detailed illustrations enabled his clients to visualise clearly his proposals. He also designed furniture, fabrics, fittings and surroundings to match his buildings.

In 1865 he set up in London and greatly expanded his business in the south of England. He was appointed assessor in architectural competitions. His son Paul became partner in 1891. Alfred retired in 1902 after a stroke, and died in 1905 at Yattenden Court, near Newbury, the third house he had designed for himself.

Waterhouse favoured picturesque styles with steep roofs and dramatic skylines, early embracing the Gothic Revival, but in Waterhousian variants. He later moved on to other styles, taking up new materials, especially ironwork, glass and terracotta. He designed few buildings of stone, preferring imaginative brickwork ranging from plain stock brick to vivid red, yellow and black. His developing use of self cleaning or washable terracotta suited smoky Victorian townscapes and created both a fashion and an industry.

Waterhouse's Quaker background meant that church building formed only a small part of his output and was mainly for Non-Conformist chapels in terracotta with unusual plans. He designed numerous country houses and villas. His public, educational and commercial buildings, however, formed prominent items in towns. His college buildings are the cores of what became the Victoria Universities of Manchester (Owens College, the Christie Library and the Whitworth Hall), Leeds (the Yorkshire College of Science) and Liverpool (College Medical Schools and Engineering

Laboratories). He rebuilt many parts of colleges at Oxford (Balliol's Broad Street frontage, Great Hall and early laboratories) and the Oxford Union. At Cambridge he built for Caius, Jesus, Pembroke, Trinity Hall and the Union and designed the new ladies college, Girton. Waterhouse was also the architect for the Prudential Assurance Company, forming an immediately recognisable corporate house style in hot red brick and terracotta in at least 27 towns between 1877 and 1901. They ranged from the London headquarters in Holborn to as far north as Glasgow and Dundee, including Newcastle upon Tyne and Darlington. The latter was completed by his son although later demolished; its statue of Prudentia will soon grace Darlington's Cornmill shopping centre.

There is a noticeable concentration of Waterhouse buildings around Darlington and in the Lower Tees Valley. By his marriage in 1860 he became related to the Quaker families and to the increasingly wealthy industrial and commercial entrepreneurs and bankers centred on the Friends Meeting House in Skinnergate, Darlington. Alfred Waterhouse married Elizabeth (Bessie) Hodgkin, the step-sister of Jonathan Backhouse Hodgkin (son of Jonathan Backhouse of Polam Hall, Darlington and husband of Mary Anna Pease of Elm Ridge, Darlington). Commissions in the region followed in quick succession.

Darlington Local Board of Health invited Waterhouse to design a new Market Hall. The result was the cast iron and glass Market Hall with the cream brick and sandstone-dressed 128 feet Clock Tower and Board Room, renamed the Town Hall on opening in 1864. The glass verandah, recently renewed, was added a little later. He built Uplands in 1862 for Rachael Pease, a daughter of Joseph Pease of Southend, in 1863 Pilmore Hall at Hurworth for Alfred Backhouse; and in 1864 Hummersknot for Arthur Pease, a son of Joseph Pease. In 1864–66 Backhouse's Bank, conspicuous on High Row, was assertively built in stone. In 1866 Hutton Hall and stables, near Guisborough, were commenced and later extended and a private railway station built for Joseph Whitwell Pease, the eldest son of Joseph Pease, both of whom were MPs. About 1867 Pendower, in Benwell, Newcastle upon Tyne, was built for John William Pease, a banker son of John Beaumont Pease of North Lodge, Darlington. Henry Pease, the younger brother of Joseph Pease, engaged Waterhouse in 1874 to embellish his mansion Pierremont in Darlington with a monumental clock tower and entrance archway, and a conservatory, grotto and sunken garden in readiness for the Golden Jubilee celebrations of the Darlington and Stockton Railway. In 1875 for J. E. Backhouse, a banker nephew of Alfred Backhouse, he designed Hurworth Grange with intriguingly-patterned red brick, now the village's community centre. In 1877 came Middlesbrough High School, now a part of Teesside University. Waterhouse designed Grinkle Park mansion near Port Mulgrave in 1882 for Sir Charles Palmer, the Jarrow shipbuilder. Mowden Hall, Darlington, was built in 1881 in hot red brick and terracotta for Edwin Lucas Pease, the third son of John Beaumont Pease of North Lodge. Guisborough Grammar School, headmaster's house and Hospital of Jesus dormitories for boarders came in 1887, and in 1895 the Mary Pease almshouses, Darlington. His elegantly simple, lofty clock tower still dominates the town centre and is now the official symbol of Darlington Borough.

Bibliography

Vera Chapman, *Rural Darlington – Farm, Mansion and Suburb*, Durham County Libraries, 1975, and High Force Publications, 1998.

Darlington Borough Planning Applications.

Dictionary of National Biography, Supplement III.

The Builder, Vol. LXXXIX, No. 3264.

The Building News, 25 August 1905,

The Buildings of England, Pevsner, Nikolaus, *County Durham* 1953; *Yorkshire: The North Riding*, 1966; Pevsner, Nikolaus and Williamson, Elizabeth, *County Durham* revised 1983; Pevsner, Nikolaus and Richmond, Ian, *Northumberland* revised 1992 by John Grundy, Grace McCombie, Peter Ryder and Humphrey Welfare. Penguin Books.

Vera Chapman

Arthur Watts (1838–1933)   Clergyman, Educationalist, Geologist

Arthur Watts, elder son of Arthur and Elizabeth (née Gutteridge) Watts, was born in Northampton, on 23 October 1838, 'of comparatively humble parents'. In 1858 he entered Cheltenham Training College and qualified as a teacher. His first post was at Burslem. During his time there he married Bertha Elizabeth White (1862). Two children were born, Elizabeth (1863) and Arthur William (1868).

141

About 1866 the family moved to Chelmsford. Besides teaching, Watts took evening classes and gave public lectures. Bertha and their baby son died in 1869.

Arthur Watts, c. 1885 (photograph supplied by D. M. Meade)

After following a course for science teachers at the South Kensington (Natural History) Museum (1870) Watts took the honours course (1871) and came top in every class. Now qualified to teach science, he was offered the post of third tutor (science and art) at the Durham Diocesan College of Schoolmasters (later called Bede College) and began work on 7 June 1871. Durham County appealed to Watts: 'From the beginning this countryside was my first text-book, and in all my teaching it took a first place years before the educational authorities began to talk about nature studies.'

Watts married Mary Ann Hearn, a gifted singer, in December. They lived at Belvedere House, Gilesgate. There were four children who survived childhood – Arthur Frank, Harry Banks, Gladys and Beatrice.

In July 1872 Watts studied biology at the South Kensington Museum under Professor Thomas Huxley. At the examination he obtained First Class Honours (with prize of books) and a brass compound microscope (for top two students). This instrument was given to his grandson when he entered medical school.

Watts was asked to introduce science at Morpeth Grammar School (now King Edward High School). He travelled the 40 miles to Morpeth and back one day a week. On relinquishing this post he became an examiner for scholarships.

Watts, with others, and the Science Department at South Kensington, established a Science School at Durham which opened in November 1873. 'Its advantages [should be] available to every energetic young man.' It taught various scientific subjects (geology by Watts) in evening classes. Successful candidates gained useful qualifications. The school led to the founding of the Johnston Technical School in 1901.

In December 1874 Watts took the licence in Theology, being ordained Deacon the following year (Priest a year later), shortly after having been promoted to the post of Vice-Principal. In 1878 he was elected as a Fellow of both the Geological and Royal Geographical Societies. For the National Society (for Promoting the Education of the Poor in the Principles of the Established Church) he wrote a science manual, *How to teach Animal Physiology* (1879).

From 1879–81 Watts acted as 'Sunday curate' at St. Giles' church (near the college). He started 'The Band of Mercy', to teach children of all denominations about nature. Activities included competitions with prizes. Moving to Shincliffe in 1881 as curate in charge, he continued to organise the Band until 1883.

In Shincliffe Watts formed a committee 'by means of which the banks and open spaces in the place were levelled and planted with trees and shrubs' (still growing today).

In November 1885 Watts prepared a petition for the release of W. J. Stead, former editor of *The Northern Echo*, then imprisoned in London for three months on a technicality, in his crusade against vice. 500 Durham people signed the petition and a separate one was forwarded from Shincliffe.

During 1887 Watts made detailed observations about pollen from 494 flowers. This formed the subject of his presidential address to the Tyneside Naturalists' Field Club in 1894 (published 1900).

In 1889 Watts was presented to the living of Witton Gilbert, three miles north-west of Durham. He continued to be present at Bede Day Festivals, walking into Durham (later using pony and trap) to celebrate 8 a.m. Communion at St. Giles' church. He was asked to address the Holy Island pilgrims in 1896, and those at Iona in 1897.

After 25 years at Witton Gilbert the parishioners presented Watts with a testimonial: 'Kimblesworth [an outlying part of the parish] has been equipped with its Mission Church, Churchyard, and Clergy House: at Witton Gilbert new buildings have been provided for the Infant Department of the National Schools, the Churchyard has been extended and greatly beautified by the erection of a Lych Gate and the liberal planting of trees and shrubs.'

Watts was widely recognised as a geologist. A London tutor advised a parish mining-engineering student to seek his help: 'He knows more about geology than most people in this country.' Watts was one of the pioneers of fighting coal-dust dangers in mines.

In 1913 he identified a neolithic stone axe, unearthed in Witton Gilbert, found a hammer equally old nearby and gave a lecture on both to the Society of Antiquaries of Newcastle upon Tyne (see its *Proceedings*, 3rd series, vol. VII, 1915–16): 'An impressive piece of work well ahead of its time' (Lindsay Allason-Jones (1999), Director of the Newcastle University Museum of Antiquities, where the 'Witton axe' is now displayed).

Watts retired in 1922 and went to live with his elder son near Gloucester. Behind the house was a quarry, rich in fossils, and he led an expedition of the Cotteswold Naturalists' Field Club there in August 1928 (see 'Excursion to Robinswood Hill' in the *Proceedings* of the Club, Vol. XXIII (2) 1928). D. V. Ager, in *Proceedings of the Geologists' Association*, Vol. 66 (1955), re certain of these fossils, wrote that Watts had 'anticipated by ten years the classic work of [L. F.] Spath [geologist, University of London] in this matter (1938).'

Arthur Watts died on 8 September 1933 and his body was brought back to Witton Gilbert for burial. A memorial window in the church commemorates him and his wife.

Bibliography

MSS in Durham Record Office, deposited by the College of St Hild and St Bede:

'Rev. A. Watts', in *Bede College Magazine*, Vol. 1, No. 3, May 1905, E/HB 2/ 559.

'Random Reminiscences of Bede College, Durham', dictated to Arthur Watts, grandson, 1933, E/HB/2/862.

'The Story of a Victorian Country Parson', by Arthur Watts, grandson (1991), deposited in DRO (Library papers) by D. M. Meade.

The Durham Chronicle, 19 September 1873; and 27 November 1885.

The Durham County Advertiser, 2 November 1883; and 15 September 1933.

Dorothy M. Meade

John Wilson (1837–1915)   M.P., Miners' Leader

W hen the Labour Party was founded in 1900, there was already a group of workers' leaders who had been in Parliament since 1880, representing the interests of the miners and other workers. Some of these MPs joined the new party, but one who remained in the Liberal Party was the Durham miners' leader John Wilson. He decided to follow the principles which had brought him into the Gladstone government, and he remained in the Liberal Party until his death.

Born in Greatham on 26 June, from the age of four when his mother died, he travelled with his father as the latter looked for employment. Although he attended many "dame schools", he was frequently punished by his father for truancy. Nevertheless he could read when six and soon was reading the classics and the Bible. This interest remained with him and he was always able to use an apt quotation in his later speeches and writing.

When John was 11, they settled in Stanhope for a while, and he began his working life in the quarries until his father died of cholera. The orphan was offered a home, and a trade, with his uncles, but he chose a life as a miner at Ludworth colliery where he had a narrow escape from a runaway tub. He next worked at Sherburn Hill where he headed a pay dispute. This marked him down as a born agitator and he was refused employment in the area.

At 19, he began a life at sea, and one voyage took him to India shortly after the Mutiny. On the return trip he caught yellow fever and was discharged. He recuperated in the village of Haswell and was nursed by the young lady he would marry. He obtained work at the nearby colliery, and showed the qualities which were to make him a labour leader.

1863 was a momentous year for John Wilson. He married Margaret Firth, daughter of George Firth, also a miner from Haswell. She stood by him in many difficult circumstances and in all his later struggles. They made the decision to emigrate to the U.S.A. where miners were in great demand during the American Civil War. They were joined by many others from the Durham coalfields. The journey, travelling steerage, was very uncomfortable and a great health risk. These miners found work in areas of Pennsylvania and Illinois. At Limetown he had his first experience of exploring and assisting after an explosion in a drift mine. During this period in the U.S.A. John and Margaret's eldest daughters were born — Dorothy and Elizabeth. Although many of the emigrants remained, the Wilson family and others decided to return to England in 1867.

Alderman Dr John Wilson, J.P., M.P.

At the age of 30, while at Haswell Colliery, John's style of life changed completely after his conversion to Christian principles. He renounced gambling and alcoholic drinks and became a member of the Primitive Methodist Church. Commencing as a Sunday School teacher, he became a lay preacher and continued this work until his death. Realising the need for self-improvement through education, he set himself a course of study, including grammar, logic, history, shorthand and theology, as well as acquiring knowledge of French and German. As a preacher, he learned the art of public speaking, and was helped in his reading by acquiring the library of a preacher who had died.

From this time Wilson was committed to the work of improving the conditions in the mines and of the miners, and he supported the growing spirit of trade unionism heart and soul. He helped to form the C.W.S. in Haswell and was on the first committee. The family soon had to move to Wheatley Hill and work was found at the colliery for a few years, until he was discharged for being an agitator and accused of inciting fellow miners to strike. He refused to leave the village and commenced a stationery business.

In 1869 he helped in the formation of the Durham Miners' Association and was elected a member of the executive 7 years later. In 1882 he became treasurer and subsequently financial secretary, and finally General Secretary in 1895 when Mr. W. H. Patterson died.

1871 saw the introduction of the Miners' Gala Day. Important speakers addressed the miners on the Racecourse, and Wilson was often one of these. Many of the Lodges paid him the honour of portraying him, with other leaders, on their Banners.

As secretary of the Durham Miners' Franchise Association, he had frequent correspondence with the Prime Minister – Mr. Gladstone – on the subject of electoral reform. Following the Household Suffrage Bill in 1885, a redistribution of seats gave Durham 8 County seats. Wilson was selected as a Liberal-Labour candidate for the Houghton division. In the ensuing election he was successful. The defeat of the Liberal government over the Home Rule Bill necessitated a further election, and this time he was defeated. Wilson referred to this Session as the 'dog watch' Parliament – the name given to two short watches at sea. The opportunity to regain a seat came in 1890 when Mr. W. Crawford died. He had represented Mid-Durham division and, in the election, Wilson held the seat with a large majority against the Tory coal-owner, Mr. Vane Tempest. He continued as the Member here until his death, on many occasions being returned unopposed.

In 1887, as a Trade Union representative on a Parliamentary deputation, he returned to the U.S.A., for the purpose of impressing upon the President the desirability of a system of arbitration between the two countries which would settle disputes without use of weapons. They were introduced to President Cleveland by Andrew Carnegie, the philanthropist and, in the following discussions, the latter was impressed by the contribution made by Wilson. When Carnegie died he left an annuity to him, but Wilson had died 4 years earlier. He made 3 further trips to the U.S.A., the first a private visit, the second in 1904 for conferences in Kansas City and St. Louis, and the last in 1911 when he was accompanied by his daughter Dorothy.

The early nineties were strenuous years for the miners' leaders and, following several crippling strikes, the Conciliation Board was established to settle wage disputes and for more than 25 years wage, and other differences, were settled by negotiation, a policy greatly advocated by Wilson. Gradually, he came into conflict with the growing ideas of Socialism, but he kept the respect of those who disagreed with him.

Courage was one of his great characteristics and this sent him to engage in the work of rescue and comfort whenever a pit disaster occurred. So it was appropriate that he acted as secretary to the Royal Commission on 'Explosions from Coal Dust in Mines'. A Parliamentary motion with which he was associated was the movement towards payment of MPs in order that the poorer members could afford to live in London during the session.

His support of the Durham Miners' Permanent Relief Fund led to a movement of great importance to him. In 1897 he backed Joseph Hopper in his pioneering work to provide free homes for aged miners, and the Aged Miners' Homes Association was formed. In this work they had the support of Bishop Westcott, who was known as the 'Pitmen's Bishop'. In all, over 300 homes were provided, scattered across the county. 26 November 1913 was a proud day for Wilson when Queen Mary visited some of the homes and he was given the honour of escorting Her Majesty.

He was a member of Durham County Council from the start in 1888, becoming Alderman and, for 3 years, its Chairman, and in 1906 he was appointed a county magistrate. On the reconstitution of Durham University, he was appointed to the Senate, and in June 1910 the honorary degree of Doctor of Civil Law was conferred on him.

In 1908 Margaret Wilson, his "life-long companion and consistent help-mate" died. This was a great blow to him and it is at this point that Wilson ends his autobiography.

Although suffering from failing health in his last years, he continued to attend the House and to preach. One of his last public functions was to open the Aged Miners' Homes at Thornley and, a week before he died, a message of sympathy on his illness was received from Queen Mary who recalled her visit to Durham.

John Wilson died on 24 March 1915 at his home by the Miners' Hall in North Road, Durham, surrounded by his only son, Christopher, and daughters Dorothy, Elizabeth, Margaret and Jane. At his funeral, three services were held simultaneously, in the Miners' Hall and two Methodist Chapels, and mourners lined North Road during the proceedings.

Bibliography

Durham Aged Mineworkers' Homes Association, 15th Annual Report, 1913.

Newspaper cuttings from *The Durham Chronicle, Evening Despatch, Sunderland Daily Echo*.

The Autobiography of John Wilson, J.P., M.P., *Memories of a Labour Leader*, Published by T. Fisher Unwin, 1910.

John Wilson, *A History of the Durham Miners' Association 1870–1904*, Published by J. H. Veitch & Sons, Durham, 1907.

Brenda P. White

Joseph Havelock Wilson (1858–1929)　　　Seaman and trade unionist

Havelock Wilson virtually single-handedly founded the National Amalgamated Sailors' and Firemen's Union, forerunner of the National Union of Seamen in Sunderland in 1887. He was born in High Street, Sunderland, in 1858, the son of a foreman draper who died when the boy was three. An errand boy at ten, then apprenticed at thirteen to a printer, he ran way to sea after only a few months, to roam the southern part of the globe for eight years.

Back home in 1879, Wilson found a new union formed – The North of England Sailors' and Seagoing Firemen's Society. In fact it was confined to Sunderland, and was a pretty inefficient organisation, but Wilson joined with enthusiasm. He had first encountered trade unionism in Australia and his experiences round the world, seeing how the seaman was cheated, starved, bullied and drowned made him an enthusiastic recruiter for the new union. It was largely run by old men who could remember the pioneering efforts of the 1850s, and their response to Wilson's passion for spreading the union to other parts was to shake their heads. Seamen, said one old leader, were a rope of sand, washed away with every tide. Wilson, meeting men from other nationally-organised unions on Sunderland Trades Council, refused to believe that.

At this time, Wilson ceased to be a seaman himself. He had married in 1879 and in 1882 he gave in to the wishes of his wife (whose father had drowned at sea) and came ashore. Together they opened 'The Wear Dining Rooms', in Church Street, Monkwearmouth, then in 1884 moved to bigger premises at the foot of High Street East, which had not only a restaurant but twelve bedrooms and a large hall at the rear. Far from giving up trade unionism, the hall for meetings was one of the great attractions for Wilson and the income security against blacklisting by employers.

J. Havelock Wilson, C.H., C.B.E., *My Stormy Voyage Through Life* (London: Co-operative Printing Society Limited, 1925) opp. p. 256

The Sunderland Union, however, was unwilling to tackle the expansion. With the assistance of a Railway Union member, Wilson drew up a rule book and in August 1887 called the first meeting of the National Amalgamated Sailors' and Firemen's Union of Great Britain and Ireland.

After that meeting there were exactly two members – Wilson and the one seaman who had turned up. At the second meeting a week later, however, there were twelve; another week and there were two hundred. At the 1888 T.U.C. Wilson represented 500 members, but only a year later there were 65,000, and 13 delegates to the Congress. This spectacular progress represents tremendous work by Wilson, travelling all over the country speaking, arguing and fighting, and in the early days spending the money his wife earned from the coffee shop to keep the union afloat. In July 1889 the union seemed secure, and then Wilson's family moved with the union head office to London, mainly to be near Parliament.

In his early days at sea Wilson had regarded Samuel Plimsoll as a hero, and always saw the creation of a union as essential if Plimsoll's campaign was to succeed. By the time the N.A.S.F.U. was established, however, Plimsoll had left Parliament, and had more or less concluded that little could be done to improve the condition of seafarers. The legislation that Plimsoll had managed to get through the Parliament in the 1870s, including the load-line of 1875, had done nothing to reduce the death toll, which reached a record level in 1881 of 3,700 deaths from wreck and accident. When the 29-year old Wilson came to him, however, he found a new lease of life, and threw himself back into the fray, and accepted the position of Honorary President of the N.A.S.F.U.

1889 was an explosive year for British trade unionism. Not only sailors were organising, but dockers, gas workers, carters, labourers – all the most exploited and underpaid whom it was believed could never form unions joined up and struck back in a wave of what has come to be called 'New Unionism'. The pent-up grievances of years broke out into strikes, and the sailors' union was among the most prominent.

No union faced more determined opposition than the seamen's. In reply to the union in 1890 the employers founded the Shipping Federation. Its aim was simply to break the union, and with the aid of a down-turn in trade, it was successful. It organised a national 'free labour' scheme, and had three ships of its own to transport and house blacklegs in striking ports. It insisted on sailors having the Federation's 'ticket', in effect giving up the union. It financed legal actions against the union and against Wilson personally, and during a dispute in Cardiff in 1891 Wilson was convicted (on very dubious evidence) of 'unlawful assembly and riot' and sent to prison for six weeks. Defeats for the union in Cardiff, Bristol and Hull ruined the organisation and finances, and in 1894 the union went into voluntary liquidation.

Immediately, a new National Sailors' and Firemen's Union was formed with Wilson as its President, but it was very weak until the upsurge of trade unionism in the years before the First World War. In 1911 the sailors, dockers and transport workers were all involved in confrontation with their employers. Solidarity brought major gains in wages, and the N.S.F.U. at last got recognition from the employers, although the seamen's war service did even more to consolidate the Union's position.

Meanwhile, even before the winding up of the original union, Wilson had gone into Parliament. Convinced by Plimsoll that only legislation would bring lasting gains, Wilson fought first Bristol in 1890 then Middlesbrough in 1892. His politics were Liberal, but the local Liberal Association would not accept him, so he stood as a Labour candidate (this was eight years before the Labour Party was formed), and became the first Labour member ever elected in a three-cornered fight. After the election, however, Wilson declared his allegiance to the Liberal Party, and he was given a free run against the Conservatives in future. He left Parliament in 1910, then was returned unopposed in South Shields in 1918, but finally lost his seat in 1922.

Not only did Wilson never join the Labour Party after its formation in 1900, he almost obsessively opposed it. In his early years in Parliament he saw his political activity as an extension of the union's industrial action. He followed up the earlier work of Plimsoll, working on committees and giving evidence to commissions and contributing to the major changes in maritime law of 1894 and 1906. From the time of the First World War, however, his fanatic anti-Germanism, followed by an obsessive fear of communism led his union further and further from the rest of the labour movement.

There were expulsions and breakaways as the N.S.F.U. grew more and more conservative and the dictatorial aspects of Wilson's character took over. To defeat his opponents Wilson used the rule-book, the courts and ordered his members to break strikes. He went so far as to use a new version of the old Federation ticket, combining with the employers to enforce a closed shop against dissident members. In 1926 Wilson and his re-named National Union of Seamen even supported the government during the general strike, then gave backing to the company unions sponsored by the coal owners to break the miners' union. In 1928 the N.S.F.U. was expelled from the TUC, and in April 1929 Havelock Wilson died at the age of 71, still President of the union he had created.

In various memoirs of employers Havelock Wilson is remembered respectfully, and even affectionately by Lord Runciman. The judgement of his fellow trade unionists was harsher. On his death *The Miner* wrote: "We do not propose to overstep the bounds of good taste in our comments upon Havelock Wilson … In his early years he performed magnificent work in organising the much ill-used seamen in this country, (but) in post-war years he has been, in plain language, a faithful ally of the employing class ... Havelock Wilson will go down in history as one of the tragedies of the twentieth century working class movement in Britain".

Bibliography

Joyce Bellamy and J. Saville, (eds), *Dictionary of Labour Biography*, 1972, vol. 4, pp. 200–208.

Obituary in *Sunderland Daily Echo*, 17 April 1929.

J. H. Wilson, *My Stormy Voyage Through Life*, 1925.

George Patterson

List of Contributors and Subjects

Professor G. R. Batho	*J. F. W. Johnston; A. E. Prowse*
Mrs Vera Chapman	*F. M. Dawson; C. M. Harker; G. G. Hoskins; J. P. Pritchett; Sir R. Ropner; N. Sunderland; A. Waterhouse*
Professor Malcolm Chase	*F. E. E. Bell; C. Duncan; H. Heavisides; J. Kane; J. Maw*
Mr Peter Davis	*Backhouse family*
Dr Sylvia Davis Furnues	*C. M. Palmer*
Dr Sheridan Gilley	*W. Hogarth*
Ms Fiona Green	*W. Falla II*
Mrs Audrey Kelly	*T. Heaviside*
Mr T. W. J. Lennard	*T. M. Greenhow*
Mr Chris Lloyd	*J. H. Bell; Sir C. W. Starmer; W. T. Stead*
Miss Dorothy M. Meade	*J. A. Chalmers; W. G. Footit; A. Watts*
Mr Donald Miller	*A. A. Byron, Countess Lovelace*
Mr W. A. Moyes	*P. Lee*
Mr Hugh Norwood	*W. S. Gilly*
Mr George Patterson	*J. Todd; J. H. Wilson*
Mrs Margaret Ray	*Sir H. Taylor*
Mr Michael F. Richardson	*F. W. Goodyear*
Miss Moira Rutherford	*T. Ramsey; H. H. Rushford*
Dr A. I. Short	*W. G. Armstrong; T. M. Greenhow*
Mr H. J. Smith	*D. S. Reid; S. Galbraith; W. Scaife*
Dr Winifred Stokes	*R. W. Jackson; C. Tennant*
Dr G. Stout	*J. Walker*
Mrs Judith E. T. Tarrant	*Rev. Canon H. B. Tristram*
Professor Michael Tooley	*W. A. Nesfield*
Mrs Brenda P. White	*J. Butterfield; J. Wilson*
Mr Alan Wilkinson	*C. Dickens; Sir W. Scott*
Professor Chris Wrigley	*A. Henderson*

DURHAM COUNTY LOCAL HISTORY SOCIETY PUBLICATIONS

(Editor: Emeritus Professor G R Batho, School of Education, University of Durham, Leazes Road, Durham DH1 1TA, Tel 0191 374 3497/8)

H T Dickinson	*Radical Politics in the Later Eighteenth Century* (1979) card covers, 24pp (members 40p) 80p
K Emsley & C M Fraser	*The Courts of the County Palatine of Durham* (1984) laminated covers, 112pp (ISBN 0-902958-07-0) (members £4.50) £7.50
D S Reid	*The Durham Crown Lordships* (1990) laminated covers, 196pp (ISBN 0-902958-13-5) (members £4.50) £7.50)
A J Heesom	*Durham City and its MPs, 1678-1992* (1992) laminated covers, 68pp (ISBN 0-902958-11-9) (members £2.50) £3.50
T Corfe (ed)	*A Historical Atlas of County Durham* (1993) laminated covers, 88pp (ISBN 0-902958-14-3) (members £4.00) £6.00
D J Butler	*Durham 1849* (1996) card covers, 52pp (ISBN 0-902958-15-1) (members £2.50) £4.00
H J Jackson	*A County Durham Man at Trafalgar, Cumby of the Bellerophon* (1997) coloured card covers, 38pp (ISBN 0-902958-16-X) (members £2.50) £4.00
Henry Green W Stokes (ed)	*Memoirs of a Primitive Methodist: Eventide Memories & Recollections* (1998) coloured card covers,44 pp (ISBN 0-902958-17-8) (members £2.50) £4.00
C M Newman	*The Bowes of Streatlam, County Durham: The Politics and Religion of a Tudor Gentry Family* (1999) coloured card covers, 32 pp (ISBN 0-902958-18-6) (members £2.50) £4.00
M Bush	*Durham and the Pilgrimage of Grace* (2000) laminated covers, 68 pp (ISBN 0-902958-19-4) (members £2.50) £4.00

Documentary Series

3   S Miller, *The River Wear Commissioners: Extracts from their papers, 1717-1846* (1980) card covers, 22pp (ISBN 0-902958-04-6)   50p

4   H J Smith, *A Mirthless Mirrour Mischievously Managed: The Dispute over the Living of Middleton-in-Teesdale, 1661* (1980) card covers, 14pp (ISBN 0-902958-05-4)   50p

5   D J Butler, *Tithe Apportionments and Maps of the City of Durham* (1987) card covers, 80pp (ISBN 0-902958-12-7)   £2.50

8   M Sobo, *Parliamentary Survey of Muggleswick, 1649* (1995) card covers, 56pp (ISBN 1-870268-21-0)   £3.00

Bulletins -   The following back numbers of Bulletin are available:-

nos.	3,6,8,913,14,25,26,27,28,29	@50p each
nos.	31,32,35	@£1.00 each
nos.	40,42,44	@£2.00 each
nos.	46,47,48,49	@£2.50 each
nos.	50,51,52,53,54,55,56,57,58,59, 60	@£3.00 each

DCLHS Publications are available from Mr D J Butler, 3 Briardene, Margery Lane, Durham DH1 4QU at the above prices plus 50p per publication for postage and packing. Cheques should be made payable to Durham County Local History Society.